PASSAGE IN CONSCIOUSNESS

A Guide to
Expanding Our Minds and
Raising the Life Forces
in Our Bodies through
Deep Meditation

JOHN VAN AUKEN

with Edgar Cayce Methods

LIVING IN THE LIGHT
VIRGINIA BEACH, VIRGINIA USA

PASSAGE IN CONSCIOUSNESS

Initial Edition
Copyright © 2008 John Van Auken
Expanded Edition
Copyright © 2016 John Van Auken

*The content in this book is
based on concepts and methods
originally taught by
Edgar Cayce
and the author's practice
for over thirty years.*

JohnVanAuken.com
John@JohnVanAuken.com

Living in the Light
P.O. Box 4942
Virginia Beach VA 23454-0942 USA

Available from
Amazon.com
and other retail outlets

CONTENTS

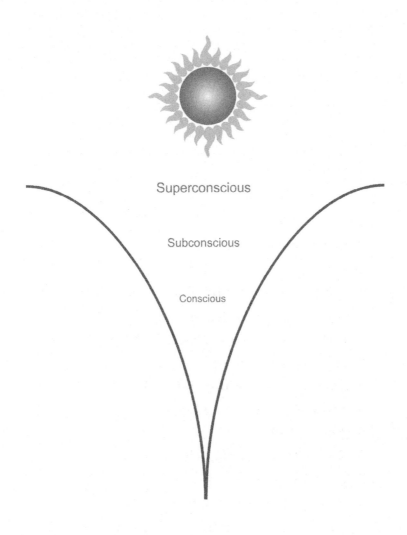

Superconscious

Subconscious

Conscious

A Note about Sources

The primary source for information in this book is from the teachings of Edgar Cayce combined with my personal practice of these concepts and methods for most of my life. And the primary source of Edgar Cayce's information was from the *Akasha*, an ancient concept that has its origin in the oldest body of religious literature yet discovered in the world, the *Ayurveda*, circa 1200 BC, a collection of "life-knowledge" written in an archaic form of Sanskrit, one of the oldest languages on Earth. In this ancient teaching *akasha* is the singular, pervading *essence* of physical substance. Yet, it is imperceptible by physical senses. Within this invisible, etheric pre-substance is every thought, feeling, vibration, word, and action in the substantial universe of physical life – and that includes us and our not-so private thoughts, feelings, vibes, words, and actions. Akasha is the *pancha mahabhuta* or "five great elements": earth, water, fire, air, and the *quintessence* (5th essence) is akasha or what you and I would understand as *ether*. *Akasha* refers to the *essence* of *manifested* life and the records of its activity since, during, and following the creation. It is a record that is recorded not in stone or on parchment. It has been referred to as "The Book of Life" or "The Book of Remembrance." It may also be thought of as a *collective consciousness* upon which all the activities and thoughts of every individual mind make an impression, an impression that can be known or "read."

There's a natural inclination to question such a imperceptible source is understandable. Nevertheless, this source gives us insights into the origins of human consciousness and the levels of the consciousness that most of us are simply not aware of in our normal state. I'll leave you the reader to discern the value of this information. But I hope that you would at least practice the method a few times before you toss it.

This akashic source was channeled by the American mystic Edgar Cayce (pronounced, KAY-see). His discourses were called "readings," because Cayce felt that he was reading the Book of Life or the Akashic Record. He was born on a farm near Hopkinsville, Kentucky, on March 18, 1877. As a child he displayed unusual powers of perception. At the age of six, he told his parents that he could see "visions," sometimes of relatives who had recently died, sometimes of angels. He could also sleep with his head on his schoolbooks and awake with a photographic recall of their contents. When he got older he developed an ability to go into a self-induced hypnotic state from which he could diagnose and prescribe healing for others. He had so much success with this that doctors around Hopkinsville and Bowling Green took advantage of Cayce's unique talent to diagnose their patients. They soon discovered that all Cayce needed was the name and address of a patient to "tune in" telepathically to that individual's mind and body and what Cayce often referred to as the "Universal Consciousness" within which all of us exist. The patient didn't have to be near Cayce, he could tune-in wherever they were. Eventually, Edgar Cayce, following advice from his own readings, moved to Virginia Beach, Virginia, and set up a hospital where he continued to conduct his "readings" for the health of others.

After some twenty years of giving only health readings Cayce began a new type of reading. It all started when one of his health inquirers asked why he had this illness, and the in-trance Cayce replied that the ailment was a karmic result of the patient's past-life misuse of the body. Well this got everyone's attention and they all wanted to know their past lives and how these were affecting them in their lives today. The new line of readings were quickly called "Life Readings." From 1925 through 1944, he conducted some 2,500 of these Life Readings. Included in these were remarkable readings about *soul life* and how every soul had been alive and active since the Creator first said, "Let there be Light." When Cayce died on January 3, 1945, he left 14,306 documented stenographic recordings of the readings given for more than 6,000 different people over a period of forty-three years. I have modernized the language, sentence structure, and syntax of his discourses to better approximate the way we read and speak the language today. It's also important for you to know that Edgar Cayce read the King James Version of the Holy Bible for every year of his life! I'm telling you this not to impress you with his spirituality but to give you an insight into why the language of many of his readings is so King-James sounding, using "thee," "thou," "ye" and the like. Another issue with some of his readings is that they can be so dense with topics and explanatory clauses as to require the reader to slow down and pay close attention to which antecedents he is referring. Of course he also gets so other-worldly at times as to be beyond our usual reality structure, requiring us to reach beyond our paradigm. And as Christian as he often was, his readings contain a many terms and concepts from ancient theologies, including ancient Egyptian, Hindu, Taoist, Mayan, and even animism.

The Edgar Cayce material is copyrighted by the Edgar Cayce Foundation in Virginia Beach, Virginia and may not be used without permission. See the copyright page in this book for details.

You, the reader, can judge for yourself whether this Akashic source combined with my personal practice are valuable to expanding your consciousness, raising the life force in your body and thusly your bodily vibrations. I found that such benefits increased my understanding and *first hand knowledge* of the *microcosm* of our finite, individual being and the *macrocosm* of infinity and the universal consciousness.

Edgar Cayce
The ring is not Masonic though he valued the Masons.

TIME magazine, August 4, 2003 issue

Foreword

The contents of this book assumes that we are celestial, spiritual beings temporarily sojourning as terrestrial, physical beings in one of the many dimensions of life. It assumes that during this incarnation we may bridge these two realities, these two aspects of ourselves and thereby enliven our temporary bodies and enlighten our immortal minds in such a manner as to become healthier, happier people who are a blessing to others and make this world a better place for us having sojourned here. It assumes that dreaming sleep and regular meditation are required practices for us to achieve this, and that our life style should include them in daily life as much as we do good hygiene, nourishment, and exercise.

A lifestyle that includes meditation as a daily or nearly daily practice can become a challenging one. This physical life can easily become all-consuming, leaving little to no room for the introspective, other-worldly practice of meditation, especially a meditation as deep as *Passage in Consciousness*. We can easily begin to think, "I just can't find time for it." Physical, outer life can influence our perspective such that say, "I just don't see the value in it." Or, since it is so

11

different from physicality we may abandon it conceding , "I'm not very good at it."

Why meditate? When we feel moody, out-of-sorts, overworked, tired, frustrated; why meditate? When we find ourselves whiny, or angry, or depressed, or weary, or any of the many feelings that human life brings; why meditate? When we can't quiet our minds because there are so many pressures, so many things that need attention; why meditate? When we are bored; why meditate? When we are sick or our loved one is sick; why meditate?

The answer to this question "Why meditate?" is both simple and complex, requiring some willpower and faith. The answer goes like this: As individuals we have only a limited amount of energy, strength, wisdom and power to effect change in our lives. As the Master asked, "Who among us, by taking thought, can change one hair on their head, or add an inch to their stature?" In the normal, human, individual condition, the answer is "None of us." But there is another condition that we CAN get into. In the universal condition, with the spiritual influences flowing, any one of us can effect change in our lives and the lives of those around us. This is the real reason for finding time and space to meditate. As a human individual we can do little, but as the universal forces find more presence within our minds and bodies, we become potent beings of the Life Force. Here are some Edgar Cayce views on this:

"As the body-physical is purified, as the mental body is made wholly at-one with purification or purity, with the life and light within itself, healing comes, strength comes, power comes." (281-24)

"So may an individual effect a healing, through meditation, through attuning not just a side of the mind nor a portion of the body but the WHOLE, to that at-oneness with the spiritual forces within, the gift of the life-force within EACH body." (281-24)

"The gift of the life-force within each body" – what a wonderful statement. Within each of us is a latent gift waiting to be claimed. It is claimed by purification of body, and the mind being wholly at-one with purity. This correlates to the passage-in-consciousness stage in which the "earthly portions" are removed from the body and suspended outside it, thereby leaving the body clear, clean, pure, so the soul can rise and the spiritual influences can penetrate the whole of our being. Then comes healing, strength and power.

"The nearer the body of an individual draws to that attunement, or consciousness, as was in the Christ Consciousness, the nearer does the body become a channel for LIFE – LIVING life – to others to whom the thought is directed. Hence at such periods, these are the manifestations of the life, or the spirit, acting THROUGH the body." (281-5)

"Let these remain as sacred experiences, gathering more and more of same – but remember, as such is given out, so does it come." (281-5)

I particularly like the explanation that many of our deep meditation experiences are the manifestations of the life or spirit acting through our bodies. After all, our bodies are atomic structures:

"The body-physical is an atomic structure. Each atom, each corpuscle, has within it the whole form of the universe – within its OWN structure. Each individual body must bring its own creative force in balance about each of the atomic centers in order for the resuscitating, revivifying to occur in the body. The law then is compliance with the universal spiritual influence that awakens any atomic center." (281-24)

It is simply a matter of natural and divine law: If we remain in the individual, human condition, then we have limited potency in dealing with life's challenges. However, if we open ourselves regularly to the "universal spiritual influence," then human conditions are tempered by these forces, and these forces are life and light, with power to make all things new.

"What moves the spirit of life's activities? GOD, but Will and Choice misdirect." (262-115)

Meditation helps our will and choice be in accord with God's. Then life's activities move in harmony and coordination with the Divine Influence.

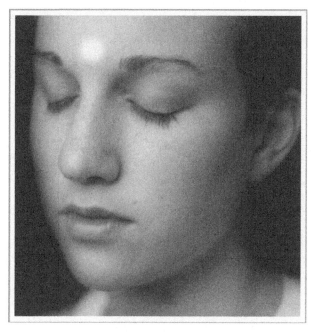

Our Meditative Sanctuary
Rejuvenates, Centers, and Enlightens

The Infinite, Universal, and Eternal
– consciousness in timeless, omnipresent, *oneness*

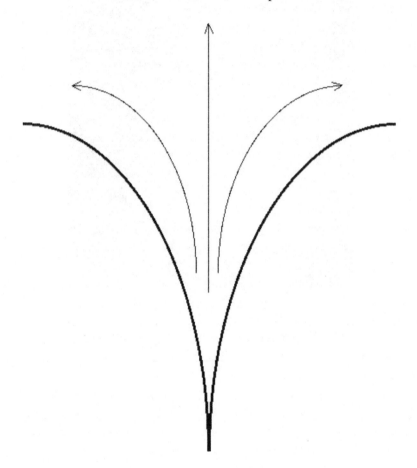

The Finite, Individual, and Temporal
– consciousness on a timeline in "manyness"

Chapter 1
PASSAGE
As Taught by Edgar Cayce

I began my journey into the Passage in Consciousness material by studying the discourses that Edgar Cayce gave for himself – the 294 series – and continued on to the 254 series, known as the "work readings," which included many readings that focused on details about Cayce's psychic process. I subsequently studied the 900, 137, and 3744 series. As I read, I began to notice that Cayce occasionally guided select individuals toward a practice he said would help them make passage *through levels of consciousness*. Although I had studied the Cayce material for many years, I had never noticed these instructions, perhaps because the method is described in bits and pieces scattered through his collection of 14,306 readings. Whatever the reason, I was surprised and pleased to have discovered something new, and I was ready to devote all the time and patience needed for the task of gathering and collating Cayce's many comments, descriptions, instructions, and intimations concerning this practice.

The practice was similar to meditation yet quite different. The 294 and 254 series of discourses helped the outer man, Edgar Cayce, to better understand the mechanics of his great ability. They describe the realms he made passage through and how his passage occurred. They explain why he couldn't always give a reading, or had difficulty in giving one, or why something strange happened during a reading[1] – all adding to my greater understanding of the nature of the process. I was even beginning to draw *maps of consciousness*, adding to them every time I found another detail.

In addition, I studied the discourses for brothers Morton (900) and Edwin (137) Blumenthal, the New York stockbrokers who were generous patrons of the Edgar Cayce work during the 1920s. Edwin's readings instructed him how to do what Cayce did, and he was told he would be able to do a better job than Cayce:

"Q. Will Edwin Blumenthal be able to give psychic readings like Edgar Cayce?

"A. The development is *beyond* those conditions as given by Edgar Cayce, for they will become conscious conditions to be acted upon by the conscious mind...."[2]

Morton, the elder brother, had a keen mind. Some of the answers to his penetrating questions for the "sleeping" Cayce gave me valuable insights into the nature of consciousness and the process of making passage through levels, planes, or dimensions of consciousness. I had already studied the Kabbalah and knew about the Seven Heavens and how to make passage through these heavens while still incarnate in this world, this dimension, so Cayce's descriptions of dimensions of consciousness or awareness were not unfamiliar to me and my practices. But his method proved to be much more effective! I had immediate success using his maps of consciousness, transitional indicators, and techniques.

The 3744 series was given for a group seeking to further understand the nature of consciousness and psychic ability. This series gives details about how the inner realms are arranged and how to journey through them while retaining some sense of awareness and sanity. Morton would often build his questions upon the answers given to the 3744 group, which helped clarify any ambiguities.

At this point you may be thinking that this was a method for giving psychic readings, but it was much more than that. By reviewing all of these discourses as a body of work, I detected that the "sleeping" Cayce was giving seekers *maps* of the inner levels of consciousness with *instructions* for making conscious, semi-conscious or unconscious (as Cayce did) passage through these realms for greater *spiritual* under-standing and discernment. Here's one example:

"The source may be from the subconscious forces of the body itself, or from the realm of spirit force as may surround the body, or a combination of both, or from a universal consciousness that is the source of life itself.... Be satisfied with nothing short of *a universal consciousness*, guided or guarded by the Lord of the Way, or the WAY itself. In Him is Life! Why be satisfied with a lesser portion than a whole measure?"[3]

In other words, we could achieve several different levels of higher awareness but the best level was the highest spiritual level from which we could gain the better perspective. I set it in my mind to seek to attune to Universal Consciousness, protected and guided by the forces I perceived to be the highest.

Why are the Edgar Cayce discourses considered the best in the world, we have this insight from the readings themselves: "...in this body lying here, Edgar Cayce, we find all life in suspension, only portions of the higher vibrations in accord with those vibrations that communicate with the *Universal* forces."[4] His ability to suspend all individual life-force and to coordinate with the higher vibrations allowed Cayce to communicate with the Universal forces. And that is ultimately what Cayce hoped would be the case for each student of this practice – a pure awareness, uncontaminated by the ego or the dark forces.

His guidance often equated *psychic* with the soul; for example, "The psychic forces are the projection of the soul development in the earth plane."[5]

Yet, these instructions encouraged passage *beyond* soul realms into the *spiritual* realms, equating spirit with God.[6] This fits well with Jesus' teaching to the woman at the well: "God is spirit, and seeks same to worship Him."[7] Readings 281-16 and -31 also correlate this practice with St. John's revelation, saying that John was in *deep meditation* when he made a breakthrough from normal consciousness into spiritual consciousness; as John said, "I was in the spirit" – and thus began his revelation.

As you might expect, I began practicing this method regularly in hopes of making a passage in consciousness of my own. At first I found the method difficult. I couldn't discern the "landmarks" of Cayce's maps of consciousness, nor could I make the transition he wanted from outer consciousness to deep inner consciousness – even though I had been faithfully meditating for more than twenty-five years at the time.

One of the first stages of the practice is to "subjugate" the physical consciousness to the control of one's soul and subconscious mind.[8] *Subjugation* literally means "to put under a yoke." I find it very interesting that the ancient Sanskrit word for *yoke* is "yoga," meaning "union." Could Cayce be selecting this word purposefully? If so, then we are to learn the yoga of setting aside our outer nature and putting it under the control of our inner nature, and finally attuning our inner nature to the Universal. Here are several quotes on subjugation:

"[When] the physical is subjugated or laid aside, we find the soul forces give the information, and the body is under the subjugation of the soul and spirit forces."[9]

"...the physical condition is subjugated to the psychical or spirit and mental forces of the body, and these produce the abnormal conditions...."[10]

"That lying between the soul and spirit forces within the entity ... is reached more thoroughly when the conscious mind is under subjugation of the soul forces...."[11]

"When the physical body lies in slumber, we find the organs [of the body] ... are subjugated, [and] the life-giving flow and the subconscious forces *acting*, and the soul forces ready for that communication."[12]

"...through the universal consciousness or cosmic consciousness from the very abilities of the entity Edgar Cayce to wholly subjugate the physical consciousness as to allow the use of the physical organs that may be attuned to all realms that pertain to psychic or mental or spiritual influences in the realms about the entity."[13]

I had spent most of my life thinking of myself as the being found in my personality and conscious mind, so it was very difficult to set this so completely aside as to turn over control to some deeper being within me and beyond my personality. It took me several weeks of practicing twice a day before I could sense this deeper me. It turned out to be extremely subtle, yet clearly distinct. Here is an early experience:

I was slowly awakening from a night's sleep, dreaming, and very much aware that I was dreaming and exactly what I was dreaming. I was very comfortable, continuing to go through the dream in my mind. Then I got up and went to the bathroom. When I returned to my bedside to write the dream in my journal, I was surprised that I could not remember the dream. It was completely gone, as though I had never had it. As I lay down, I began to do the passage in consciousness practice in an effort to recapture the dream, as well as understand how I could have lost it so quickly and completely. When I got to a certain level in the practice, and as though from out of nowhere, the dream came to me. This was a clear example of the distinction between the inner me, who had had the dream and with whom I was very comfortable, and the outer me who did not have the dream but took control of consciousness when I moved the body to the toilet. I didn't remember the dream because the me that is in charge of moving the body is not the me who had been dreaming.

For the first time I realized just how thin yet opaque the veil is between these two levels of consciousness. And the shift in consciousness was so subtle that I didn't notice it. I was not able to discern when I was in one consciousness and not in the other. I also realized how familiar I was with my inner self, my soul. It was *me*. When in the dreaming state I was comfortable and felt this was clearly me. Yet the two "me"s were distinct – even the contents of their minds was different.[14] When I was in my dreaming self, I considered it to be *me*. I said, "*I* am dreaming." When I was in my outer, everyday self, I also considered it to be *me*. Yet these parts of my being with which I was familiar and comfortable were separate and distinct.

As I learned to discern the outer me from the inner me (my personality from my individuality or soul) the practice began to take off. I began to see and feel what Cayce was teaching. Subjugation of the personality and conscious mind to the individuality (soul) and the subconscious mind was becoming a clearer, more identifiable shift or "turning," as the apostle John described it in beginning his Revelation.[15]

In 3744-1 we are told, "With the submerging of the conscious to the subconscious, *the personality of the body and/or the earthly portions are removed and lie above the other body.*" "Above the body" is because Cayce always laying on his back when giving a reading. When one is sitting up the earthly portion is removed and suspended in front of the body.

On one occasion in New York City, Cayce was giving a "World Affairs" discourse for a group of people that were sitting in a circle around his supine body. While the reading was going on, one of the participants wrote another question on a piece of paper and reached across Cayce's "sleeping" body to hand the question to the conductor, but he struck something above Cayce's body that no one in the room could see. When he hit this invisible something, the reading stopped and Cayce's body rose straight up onto his feet like a board, his hands still over his solar plexus. It was as though pulleys had raised him up to his feet, for his legs and back did not bend, and he rose stiff from the couch to a standing position. Some thought it was like levitation.[16] An event like this one happened again but Cayce's physical body almost turned a somersault; his head bent over to where his feet usually were. The witnesses rolled him back over and kept trying to give him the wake-up suggestion. Eventually, he awoke feeling fine.[17]

Cayce got a follow-up reading that explaining that the reactions were caused "by the mere disturbing of the body that rests *above* the natural body." Apparently, when Cayce removed his personality and

25

earthly portions of his body, they became what he referred to as a *thought-form* body, and remained connected with his physical or "natural" body. If one struck or disturbed his thought-form body it dramatically affected his physical body.

The readings explain that Cayce removed these aspects of himself from his physical body so that his soul and deeper mind could move more freely within the body temple with its spiritual centers and pathways [more on these in Chapter 4] into the Universal Consciousness. Cayce said humanity didn't even use personality in the early periods on Earth (Lemuria and Atlantis). This was a development that came later as the Morning Stars (our souls, see the biblical book of Job 38:7) pushed their way deeper and deeper into matter. When entities met in the early periods on Earth, they were actually speaking directly to one another's soul, to the whole of their being. Personality is of *this* material dimension, Cayce says, and so he removes the personality and the earthly portions.[18] For Cayce it was the earthly Edgar Cayce, which needed to get out of the way for the purer communication to occur.

As I continued practicing – and to my great surprise – I too began to feel this removal and suspension of my personality and earthly portions above or in front of my physical body (depending on whether I was lying down or sitting up). For the first several months I would lie down during each session. Later, when doing the practice sitting up, I'd feel my personality and earthly portions in front of my body.

It was quite amazing to realize that personality is such a small portion of the total me. Cayce: "When the subconscious controls, *the personality is removed* from the individual, and only other forces in the trinity [are] occupying the body and using ... its elements to communicate, as in this body here [Edgar Cayce's]."[19]

The Cayce readings explain that in the early periods personality development occurred because of a shift from *inner conception* (as the legendary Isis conceived Horus, Kaushalya conceived Rama, and the ancient Chinese legend that a virgin-mother conceived all humanity) to *outer conception or breeding* (as Adam and Eve conceived Cain and Abel). Ultimately, Mary, the mother of Jesus, reawakened to this ability in conceiving Jesus as the archangel Gabriel explained, "the power of the Most High will overshadow you."[20] Spiritual beings could conceive material bodies using energy to affect matter.[21] Earthly humans breed by attracting another physical body to join with them. Therefore, humans want to project an appealing *outer* body and *personage,* or what we have come to know as personality. This union of consciousness to a projected aspect of oneself drew us out into a more narrow personage. Thus, consciousness of the deeper aspects of our being were submerged in the "un-" or "sub-" conscious, virtually lost to the conscious self.

Understanding this key little concept changed my consciousness. I was breaking open to new vistas with almost every practice. Yet I noticed in my everyday life that certain activities or people could quickly pull me back into my personality. When this happened I became more narrowly focused, experiencing life from self only. However, when I was in my individuality (my soul self), my feelings and thoughts were more holistic. It seemed that I wasn't so self-centered but more collectively sensitive to all life.

I also began to experience some of the *physical* changes that accompanied Cayce's readiness to give a reading. Just as Gertrude Cayce watched for Edgar's breathing to become deep and his eyes to begin the "rapid eye movement" (REM) associated with entering the dream state, so I noticed that my "turning" from outer consciousness to inner consciousness was accompanied by *a shift in my breathing pattern* and *stimulation to my closed, carnal eyes* – as though they were seeing something while yet closed. When Cayce's breathing had shifted, his eyes were in REM, and his personality had been removed, Gertrude would give the suggestion to his subconscious to give the information being sought, and his soul would begin the passage to get the requested information. It was also at this point that I would know that I had indeed subjugated my outer self to my inner self's control, and I would give myself the suggestion to begin the next stage.

The next stage is to *raise the subconscious to a higher level*, expanding toward universal or God consciousness. As one moves closer to this level, one has to do with the individuality and subconscious mind what was done with the personality and conscious mind – subjugate *them* to the control of one's spirit being and *superconscious* mind.

Now here's where consciousness gets very uncertain. Edgar Cayce was *not* conscious of this transition. When he gave a discourse, his outer self was not be aware of any of the inner experience. Edwin Blumenthal was told that he "would be able to bring same to consciousness from the physical standpoint" and his conscious mind would be able to act upon the experience and guidance gained. Of course, he was told that this would not occur immediately – there would at first be "lapses" in consciousness, then semi-consciousness, but eventually *total* consciousness of the entire process. Edwin had a tendency to resist lapsing in consciousness, trying not to fall asleep. But discourse 137-5 told him "not [to] warn or fight against [these lapses] when entering the silence, and through such lapses will the first development show." Cayce also instructed seekers not to "build barriers" that the subconscious would have to overcome, but "lend the assistance to the subconscious forces to direct."[22]

Morton thought the spirit and its companion, the superconscious mind, would descend into the earthly consciousness, but the readings said the opposite was required. One had to *ascend* into the superconsciousness, otherwise one would only experience the projections from these higher realms. Here are some highlights from this discussion:

"Q: What is this spirit entity in the body, Morton Blumenthal, and how may he develop it in the right direction?

"A: This is only the portion that develops other than in earth's plane. Spirit entity. For soul's development is in the earth's plane – the spirit entity in the spirit plane.

"Q: Does the spirit entity have a separate consciousness apart from the physical, and is it as the consciousness of Morton Blumenthal when he dreams, or has visions, while asleep?

"A: The spirit entity is a thing apart from any earthly connection in sleep ... the earthly, or material consciousness is ever tempered with material conditions; [while] the superconsciousness, the consciousness between soul and spirit, ...partakes of the spiritual forces principally. In consciousness we find *only projections* of subconscious and superconscious, which conditions project themselves in dreams [and] visions, *unless [one] enters into the superconscious forces.*

"Q: Does the spiritual entity, after leaving this earth's plane, have full realization of the physical life or experience through which it passed while on earth's plane?

"A: It may, should it choose."[23]

Associated with this transition from soul to spirit, and from subconscious mind to superconscious, the readings explain that there is a recognizable sensation of "expansion" and "universalization."[24] It wasn't long before I knew what the readings were talking about. I felt as though I had opened the door from the finite world to the infinite universe. My mind felt as though it rapidly expanded, containing a portion of everything that ever existed. I could see how Cayce could get information on just about anyone and anything. Physically, I noticed my head being drawn back and my body extending as though it too were expanding. The readings identified these sensations as indicators of progress.[25]

From this point on, one actually "leaves" the microcosm of "an entity," as the Cayce discourses call it, and enters into the Universal forces, or aspects of God's being. The first level is the Universal Mind and the Personal God. According to the discourses, this is also the level of the "Communion of Saints" or

"Community of Seekers."[26] Often Cayce's spirit would ascend to this high level of consciousness to receive the "Book of Life" for someone seeking a reading. The "Keeper of the Records" would give him the book and often guide him as to what should or should not be read.[27] Occasionally, other discarnate souls or spirits would help with the discourse, or even contribute their own perspective or advice.

If you are familiar with Cayce's description of his own passage in consciousness, you know that in the lower levels of consciousness (lower realms of the soul) discarnate souls were trying to distract him from his mission. At the middle levels (realms of the better souls) Cayce would see others living life as though there had been no death. These souls neither distracted him nor helped him. Then Cayce would reach a higher level of consciousness (the spiritual realms) in which souls would help him with his mission. At this higher level, as I said, we come into the Communion of the Saints, the Community of Seekers, and the collective consciousness of all those who love God-consciousness and have attuned themselves to God or the source of the Life Forces.

One of the keys to Edgar Cayce's success with making direct passage through dimensions of consciousness into the Universal Consciousness was the use of a powerful suggestion to do so.[28] Cayce rarely recommended books, but one he did recommend was *Laws of Psychic Phenomena* by Dr. Thomson Jay Hudson, Ph.D., LL (1892); and the first law is that the subconscious is always amenable to a suggestion.[29] This is best done as we feel the subjugation of control to the subconscious occurring. At this point in the practice the subconscious is present and receptive to suggestion. Remembering that Cayce said the subconscious is the mind of the soul,[30] I used this suggestion (and still do): "Arise my soul and expand into the spirit and mind of God – the infinite, universal mind and spirit of God." I would *imagine* God's infinite nature until I could *feel* it. It was expansive, vast, all-inclusive. Eventually, I would feel myself expanding into this infinite, universal condition, leaving all individual, finite sensations behind. Then, I would connect with God completely. I actually felt like I was expanding into God, becoming infinite and undefined as a person. God and I were one. Not that I was God, but rather that I was completely within and one with God. At this point I stopped directing the practice and became *receptive* to God's spirit and mind. Cayce warned that we may have a tendency to tell God how best to enliven and enlighten us. We must resist this urge. Therefore, I was and am careful to become receptive, no longer driving the practice. I use the affirmation that Cayce recommended: "Not my will but Thy will be done in and through me." I then allow and imagine or even feel God flow into me. It was and remains an amazingly rejuvenative, revitalizing, revivifying experience – like plugging into the electrical power source of the Universe and being recharged!

Knowing *when* to do things in the practice is important. Waiting to give the suggestion until one can sense that subjugation of control to the subconscious is happening, as indicated by a shift in your breathing pattern, is vital. Therefore, when I feel my breathing getting deeper or simply "shifting," then I give myself the suggestion. I repeat it over and over, not by rote, but with feeling and expectancy, until I feel the rising and expanding into the Infinite, the Universal. Then I connect completely, or "plug in." This is the stage where I stop using the suggestion and begin the affirmation, "Not my will but Thy will be done in and through me." Then I imagine and ultimately feel the Infinite, the Universal flow into me. At some point, I feel filled with the spirit and mind of God, and "flow" shifts to *oneness, peace,* and *stillness.* I abide in this with out moving until something indicates that this practice session is ending.

The *imaginative forces* are useful when attempting to make passage in consciousness. Cayce often referred to these as helpful and important to reaching beyond the physical.[31]

As my practice has developed and I have become consciously aware of reaching the Universal level, I too feel the interconnectedness of everything or the "relativity of all force," as 3744-1 describes it. With the subtlest inquiry I feel I can receive a universal response. It is a wonderful place for a predominantly material person to be even *partially* conscious – just *being* there energizes and renews me. I come back nourished, comforted, and at complete peace with myself and my life. At the same time I am fired up with the determination to fully realize this expansiveness in my *entire* consciousness, integrating all levels of my being into one wonderful, fully interconnected whole.

In some of his readings Cayce indicated that our spiritual selves have known this level of attunement and oneness before – but chose to leave it. This always troubled me. I watched carefully to see if I would begin to drift away even after experiencing the Presence of God directly. Sure enough, it was amazing how outer life and self-interests gradually, subtly crept into my consciousness, and before long I was back into physical life with all its activities and stimulations, and not setting aside time for the attunement. Now, I simply do not let my outer self's fascinations with the world eliminate the budgeted time for attunement. It's a discipline, a very important and worthwhile discipline.

One of the most immediate results of this practice was a marked increase in my dreaming, dream recall, and a heightened vitality in my dreams. It was as though my outer self had made a breakthrough into the world of my inner self, and now my inner self was going to make a breakthrough into my outer world, as well. More on this in Chapter 3.

REVIEW OF THE STEPS

Let's review the fundamental steps of this practice:

Removing the earthly portion and the personality is first step in each session. This leaves the body open and free of lower levels of being and consciousness.

Turning over control of the whole system to the subconscious mind and the soul-self is the next important step. When the systems are under subjugation to the soul and subconscious, the breathing pattern will shift. This is the time to give the subconscious the *suggestion* to rise up and expand into the higher consciousness and vibrations.

The spirit realms are more expansive than the lower realms, and we will feel ourselves expanding as we rise into these higher realms – as indicated by the V-shaped diagrams on pages 4, 10, 43, and 46. The lower levels are focused at the bottom tip of the V, and the higher realms are at the expansive top of the V. As we feel ourselves moving into the infinite, universal dimensions of God's presence, we must make a complete connection and shift from the *directive* suggestion to the *receptive* one: "Not my will but Thy will be done in and through me." Then, allow the Infinite to flow into us. Eventually, we will feel one with the Infinite – and abide in this oneness until there is an indication that the session is ending.

Cayce explains that in order for this practice to reach its full potential, we must *live* our outer lives in a manner *reflecting* our inner attunement. We cannot be attempting to tune to God while cursing, hating, or ignoring everyone around us. These are not separate realities. They are one. We may be separating and defining them for the purpose of greater understanding and awareness but, as Cayce would often say at the end of his readings on these levels of consciousness, they are one. Indeed separation and oneness existing simultaneously is a paradox. It's like the paradox of believing our privacy and separateness from the All-Knowing, All-Present Mind of God. We certainly feel alone, but there is truly no way we can be outside of the Whole or even separately alone within its all-knowing mind. Yet, it certainly feels that way. Cayce explained that "the individual becomes lost IN the Whole."[32] Then he instructs us to live this new awareness and energy in our life and among the lives of those share life with.

This practice expands our awareness and raises our bodily life forces.

"Do the difficult things while they are easy and do the great things while they are small. A journey of a thousand miles must begin with a single step."
–Lao Tzu

Chapter 2
STEP-BY-STEP GUIDE
For Making Passage in Consciousness

Here are the major steps:

Select a place and budget a time for the practice. Go to that place and time daily or near daily. Allot a minimum of 30 minutes, preferably an hour – honestly, any amount of time would be better than no time set aside for practicing.

Begin with stretching exercises. Stretch by reaching up high with your arms and hands while on your tiptoes. Alternate reaching to the ceiling with one hand then the other, like a cat stretching on a carpet. After a few of these stretches, bend over and touch your toes, stretching your joints, limbs, and spinal column. Continue the alternating motion with these toe-touching stretches. Now, do the Cayce head-and-neck exercise: tilt your head forward, touching your chin to your chest. Feel the stretch down your back and spine as your head goes forward. Do this slowly three times. Now, left up your chin and tilt your head back three times, feeling the stretch down the front of your body and spine. Now, tilt the head to the right shoulder three times, feeling the stretch down the left side. Then, tilt it to the left shoulder three times, feeling the stretch down the right side. Now, rotate the head three times clockwise and then three times counterclockwise. The key is to feel the stretches all the way down your spine.

Now, do Cayce's breathing exercise: Deeply inhale through your right nostril by pressing your left nostril closed with your finger, filling your lungs, and feeling strength throughout your body as you inhale. Hold the breath for a moment. Then, exhale slowly and completely through your mouth. Pause with empty lungs for a moment. Then, repeat the inhalation through the right nostril, filling the lungs, and feeling strength. Do a total of three of these breaths. Next, inhale through the left nostril while feeling yourself opening to the Source of Life (press your right nostril closed with your finger). Hold the breath for a moment. Exhale slowly through the right nostril, not the mouth, by pressing your left nostril closed with your finger. Pause with empty lungs for a moment. Do this breath three times. During the first part of this breathing exercise (inhaling through the right nostril and exhaling through the mouth) you should feel strength, during the second part (inhaling through the left nostril and exhaling through the right nostril) you should feel uplifting and opening of the spiritual forces of the body. It's good to have fresh air in the room while doing this breathing exercise to bring more oxygen into the circulatory system and brain.

Now, get in a relaxed position you can maintain for the whole session. If you decide to lie down, then you must cover your solar plexus with your hands (this is Cayce's instruction). If you decide to sit up, then you do not have to be concerned with this. Place your hands wherever they are most comfortable - in your lap or on your legs, palms up or down or cupped together. It's up to you. But when lying down, you must cover your solar plexus.

From here on you will need your imaginative forces.

Imagine the following:

Remove your earthly portions and personality from your body. With your mind's eye, see your mental hands moving the earthly portions and personality out of your body to a place in front of your body. Hold them there. You can let them back in later. For now you are clear of them. Your body feels lighter and open, ready for your soul to come forth.

Now, subjugate control of your body to your soul and subconscious mind. They are perfectly capable of handling this assignment. See, feel, know your soul and subconsciousness mind are taking control of the system. An indication that this is occurring is a shift in your breathing, usually to deeper, steadier, slower breathing. Feel yourself turning over control to your subconscious and soul.

Once you feel the subjugation and deeper breathing, inspire your soul and subconscious to ascend and expand into the mind and spirit of God, the Universal Consciousness and Infinite Spirit. Use a directive suggestion, such as: "Arise my soul and enter into the Presence of God, the Mind and Spirit of God; the infinite, universal consciousness of God." Feel yourself rising up, feel the expansiveness and the buoyancy of the spirit of the Source of all life. Direct yourself to become universal and infinite. Imagine it. See it. Feel it. Know it is happening.

Draw your head back slightly and allow your soul and subconscious mind to expand through dimensions of consciousness – upwardly and outwardly expanding into God's infinite presence. Keep the "movement" upward and outwardly expanding until you feel yourself becoming a part of the whole of the universal consciousness, like a drop of water becoming aware of the ocean of water within which it exists.

When you sense the infinite presence of God, connect with It. Plug into It. Hold on and maintain a connection with It. Attune yourself to the Infinite Oneness or God. Then, shift from seeking hard and guide yourself to becoming receptive to God's will. Use an affirmation, such as: "Not my will but Thy will be done in and through me." Feel God's will, God's Spirit, flowing into you. Allow it to permeate every cell of your body, every portion of your mind, every aspect of your soul. (Despite the thrill of it, you must try to subdue emotion and personalness. Stillness and universalness are necessary for ideal attunement.)

Once your body, mind, and soul are fully imbued with this Life Force, abide silently there. Attempt to stay conscious or at least semi-conscious. If sleep overtakes you, awake slowly, sensing your deeper mind's perceptions rather than your outer mind's. At first, this may be difficult. Losing consciousness, like falling asleep, is a natural tendency at this stage. But eventually, you'll be able to maintain consciousness. Your breathing may be very shallow, almost not moving. Abide here. Cayce says that there is a magic in this silence. Allow that magic time to do its work.

When you sense that the session is concluding, then gradually begin to make your way back into physical life, bringing with you the spirit, energy, and essence of this attunement, this oneness with the Infinite. Feel yourself moving back into the body. Take a deep breath to aid you in drawing yourself back into the body. But bring the spirit, energy, and essence of the attunement. Take another breath and draw the higher self back into the body and this dimension of life.

Now, begin to balance the energies for proper functioning in physical life by equally distributing the energy throughout your body, not leaving supercharged energy in the upper portions (the head, neck, and shoulders). Imagine moving the energy to every portion of your body and mind – balanced, equally distributed. Cayce said that the internal organs of the body play a role in this balancing. Feel the energy in your lungs, liver, kidneys, intestines, glands, and skin. The brain is already full of energy. Let the energy now move from the brain to the other organs in order to regain equilibrium. This is an important step. Cayce suffered physically when he did not do this rebalancing. Take time to do it well.

Now let your daily actions, thoughts, and words reflect your attunement, not in a pious or better-than-thou manner, but in a natural, loving, cooperative manner. Watch your dreams. This practice will ignite dreaming. (Tips on dream recall and interpretation are in Chapter 3.)

With a little practice we can deeply attune ourselves to God and retain that spirit, energy, and essence in our daily lives.

As you can see by the technique, it does require some time. Cayce advised setting aside an hour for the practice. In the first year that I practiced this it would take me about thirty minutes to see, feel, and know the first nine steps; now it takes about five minutes, leaving the rest of the time to be in the universal, infinite condition. Rebalancing also used to take much longer than it does now. Sometimes I would find myself an hour later still "out of it" and with energy in my head. Nowadays, just the realization of this seems to distribute it, and my body seems to know how to do this quickly. Training. The more you practice, the more you develop your body, mind, and spirit to know and understand the finite condition and the infinite condition. There was a time when I thought I would be walking around with a glowing aura and radiating a higher vibration, but the overall experience is really quite natural and normal when balanced and integrated into your life and the whole of your being. One can be here, projected into individualness, or there, expanded into universalness. After a while, even when in individualness you feel the universalness. It's wonderful but much more natural and normal than I expected. However, Cayce always taught that it would be, saying that we were in the infinite, universal condition prior to incarnating into this dimension, this world. Therefore, returning to the other condition will not feel supernatural but natural.

I usually practice once or twice a day, in the morning and evening. Most often I practice in my bed as I'm preparing to sleep for the night. As the session

45

ends, I let myself fall asleep. This works well, as long as you are not so tired that you cannot maintain consciousness long enough to reach oneness with God. The morning session has more energy and vitality to it, leaving me charged-up for the day. Nowadays, I can complete the full process in about twenty to thirty minutes, sometimes faster. But every few days I stay in the deeper condition for an hour. It always allows the "magic silence" to better imbue me with the vitality, peace, and clarity of God's spirit and mind.

Cayce warned that it is important to apply this experience in everyday life. Outer life is important to your soul's mission here. We must be up and doing, experiencing life and helping others. Cayce often instructed us to let God come through us into this dimension, into the lives of people around us. Not in a pompous manner but by naturally applying the fruits of the spirit: kindness, gentleness, patience, understanding, etc.

Maps of Consciousness & Being
Levels of *Consciousness*

In the following illustration we see the three levels of our consciousness or mind: conscious, subconscious, and superconscious. As the V-shaped diagram indicates: these three levels begin with the very narrow, focused level of our earthly, three-dimensional conscious mind which is incarnate in an individual body, expands upward and outward through our fourth-dimensional subconscious mind which is the mind of our soul-self, and on to the superconscious level of our mind which is so closely connected to God's infinite, universal mind. The superconscious mind was made in the image of the Creator, God, and is the closest aspect of our mind to God's mind. As the V-lines-arrows indicate, rising upward through levels of mind or consciousness expands us from a point of awareness in a single body at the tip of the V-shape to an expansive, collective consciousness that is in the oneness of all life.

As Cayce explains, during the practice we do not draw the superconscious down to our level of consciousness, but rather lift ourselves up to its level of consciousness. The process is one of expansiveness and uplifting, of moving from individualness to universalness. It feels like moving from a point of consciousness to an expansive consciousness in the oneness with all life, all consciousness. Therefore, you can see how Cayce would have been able to access anything or anyone to give one of his now famous readings. The practice begins with setting aside the conscious mind and its earthly concerns, giving a powerful suggestion to the subconscious mind to rise up into the universal, infinite mind of God – where our superconscious mind is able to perceive. As a session ends we are to bring this perception back with us, imbuing the two other levels of mind with its essence and guidance.

See illustration on page 49.

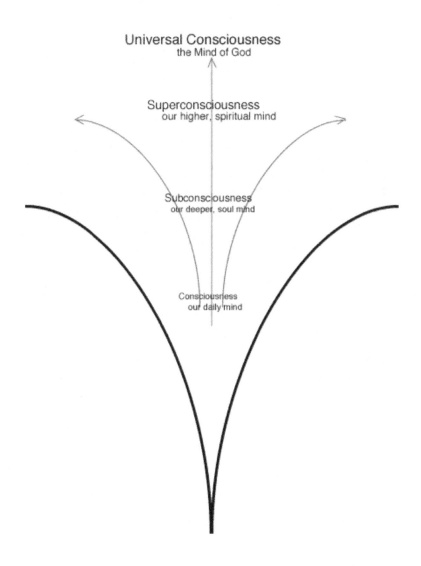

Maps of Consciousness & Being
Levels of *Being*

In the following illustration we see three levels of our being: personality, soul, and godling. As the V-shaped diagram indicates: these three parts begin with the very narrow, focused level of our personality, which is incarnate in an individual body, expands upward and outward through our soul-self, which is the individuality of our deeper self, and on to the broad, universal level of our spiritual, godling nature. The godling was made in the image of the Creator, God, and is the closest aspect of our being to God's infinite, universal nature. As the blue lines indicate, rising upward through our levels of being expands us from a point of consciousness in a single body at the tip of the V-shape to an expansive, collective consciousness that is in the oneness of all life.

Cayce explains that the personality is a temporary development of being used during an incarnation in the physical realm. After death it is absorbed into the soul-self, where it becomes an added dimension to our deeper self. The soul-self is the eternal, developing portion of ourselves that is destined to become a companion to God. It has all the memories of our journey from the dawn of creation and continues to seek out opportunities to develop itself for companionship with the Infinite Creator. The godling self is the same yesterday, today, and tomorrow. It is ever before the throne of God and does not partake of anything earthly. We must lift ourselves up into its level of being in order to experience it. It does not descend to our level. The earthly self is set aside or removed from the body during the practice. The soul-self is inspired by a strong suggestion to rise up and enter into the spiritual self and its connection with God. As a session concludes, we bring the essence of the godling connection back with us, imbuing even the outer personality with a sense of our godling self. In this way all three parts of our being are integrated, eventually becoming one with each other and with God.

See illustration on page 52.

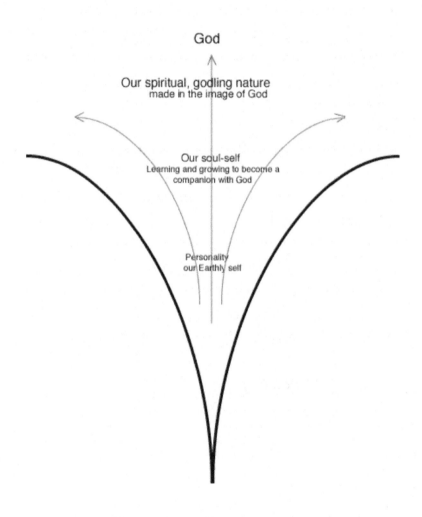

God

Our spiritual, godling nature
made in the image of God

Our soul-self
Learning and growing to become a
companion with God

Personality
our Earthly self

Maps of Consciousness & Being
Levels of the *Macrocosm*

According to Cayce's travels through the levels or dimensions of life, both within himself and within the dynamics of all life, there is a macrocosm for the passage and a microcosm. As the terms indicate, one is a map of the inner self's passage (micro) and the other is a map of all life's passage (macro).

In the following illustration we see that souls are living on three basic levels: incarnate in the Earth, discarnate in the dimensions of soul-life, and in the community of the saints or seekers in heavenly, spiritual dimensions. As Cayce began his passage he sensed the borderland between this world and the next. Here he became aware of many discarnate souls of varying degrees of attunement, mostly attempting to distract him, even possess him. He maintained his focus on his mission and purpose, not letting them distract him. As he moved beyond them, he became aware of many dimensions of soul-life beyond the borderland where discarnate souls were living dynamic lives. He noticed that in these realms there was light but it was not the light of the sun, and there was no night, no sleep. These souls occasionally noticed him but did not attempt to distract him. Eventually, he made his way up into the heavenly realms where there seemed to be a community of seekers or "saints" that began to help him with his task.

During Cayce's experience with these dimensions he noticed souls moving up and down, like biblical Jacob's dream of a ladder to heaven, upon which angels were ascending and descending through the many levels of life.

As the diagram indicates, the lower level is very focused into a point of being and mind in one body, expanding as one rises upward through the dimensions.

For Cayce, it was very important that we keep a strong sense of purpose for making passage, seeking only to connect with God's presence. From there, if God guides us to perceive other dimensions, then that's fine. But we don't want to be seeking these other dimensions without full attunement to God. It only leads to trouble and distraction. Seek God first, and then other dimensions may gradually become available and meaningful to our full understanding and service.

See illustration on page 55.

The Macrocosmic Map

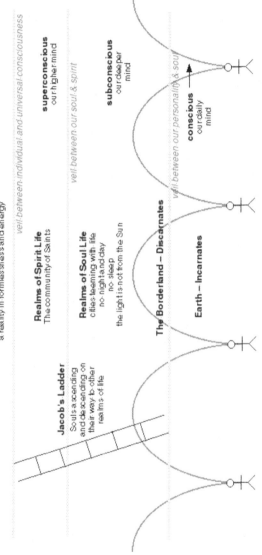

The Realm of Oneness
Infinite - Universal
a reality in formlessness and energy

veil between individual and universal consciousness

superconscious
our higher mind

Realms of Spirit Life
The community of Saints

veil between our soul & spirit

subconscious
our deeper mind

Realms of Soul Life
cities teeming with life
no night and day
no sleep
the light is not from the Sun

conscious
our daily mind

veil between our personality & soul

Jacob's Ladder
Souls ascending
and descending on
their way to other
realms of life

The Borderland – Discarnates

Earth – Incarnates

The Realm of Individualness and Separation
a reality in form and matter

55

Maps of Consciousness & Being
Levels of the *Microcosm*

In the following illustration we have the levels of the microcosm showing how an individual lives on four basic levels of life: 1. incarnate within a physical body with a three-dimensionally conscious mind, 2. in an expansive dimension of soul and subconscious mind, 3. in the even more expansive dimension of spirit and superconscious mind, and ultimately, 4. beyond individualness altogether, attuned to the Whole of the Cosmos in oneness with all life.

As one moves up these dimensions he or she encounters veils or barriers between the levels. It requires practice and heightened sensitivity to perceive and make passage through these veils.

The outer or lowest realm is in form or what we call matter. The inner or higher realm is formless or pure energy. But this is not the type of energy we usually think of. It's comparable to the more subtle energy found within our bio-electrical bodies. This is the energy or spirit of our subtler nature, our heavenly nature. We are matter and energy, physical and spiritual. The soul and subconscious mind are the bridging aspects of our being that help us experience in these two different conditions.

See illustration on page 57.

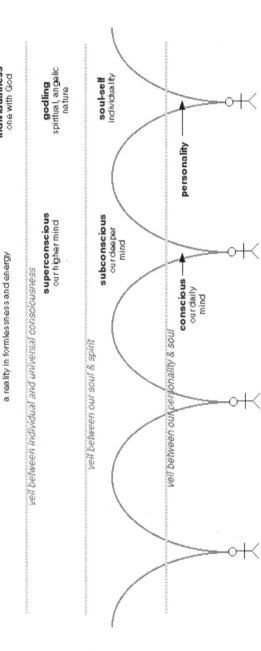

The Microcosmic Map

The Realm of Oneness
Infinite - Universal
a reality in formlessness and energy

veil between individual and universal consciousness

veil between our soul & spirit

veil between our personality & soul

beyond
individualness
one with God

godling
spiritual, angelic
nature

soul-self
individuality

superconscious
our higher mind

subconscious
our deeper
mind

conscious
our daily
mind

personality

The Realm of Individualness and Separation
a reality in form and matter

"Why does the eye see a thing more clearly in dreams
than the imagination when awake?"
–Leonardo da Vinci

Chapter 3

IN THE ARMS OF MORPHEUS

Death, Sleep, Dreams, and the Sixth Sense

Death is the ultimate change in consciousness. According to ancient Egyptians, death causes the *ba* (soul) to leave the physical body and begin its journey through the *netherworld* or underworld on its search for the heavens. Prior to entering the underworld the soul's heart is weighed in the balance as the gods look on. If the heart is light, then the soul may continue its journey through the underworld up to the heavens. If the heart is heavy, then the soul has "unfinished business" that weighs down its ability to make the passage up to the heavens, so it wanders in the underworld seeking an opportunity to rise with the sun on a new morning; some believe it reincarnates in order to have an opportunity to lighten its heart by resolving unfinished business.

A soul seeking its way through the underworld to the heavens gets help from the god Anubis, a jackal-headed god, who shows the way. The jackal head represents the unique ability of a canine (dog, jackal) to pick up the scent of a trail when we have become lost and cannot find our way home – our heavenly home. This is an important god in ancient Egypt because it can always picks up the scent of the way back to heaven. Legend holds that the children of God have lost their way and cannot recall or pick up the scent of their way into this world. The "sixth sense" of Anubis can find the way and lead the spiritual children back home. In this metaphorical story, the *underworld* is representative of the *unconscious* and the heavens represent *higher consciousness*. It was believed in ancient Egypt that the Nile represented the barrier between the land of the incarnate "living" and the land of the "living dead." Thus, crossing the Nile was like crossing the barrier of the dark unconscious and finding light and life on the other side.

Nicodemus once asked Jesus to reveal to him the hidden, metaphysical secrets, and Jesus gave him three secrets, of which this was one: "No one ascends to heaven but he or she who descended from it, not even the Son of Man." (John 3) Within us is a part of our greater being that descended from heaven and is seeking its way back home. At the Last Supper Jesus tells his disciples that they *know* where he is going and the way, but the disciples reply that they neither know where he is going nor the way. (John 14)

Deep within all of us is the sixth sense, "the knowing." It simply has to be awakened.

This has been the story of death, and for our purposes here we need to know that sleep is a shadow of death. We don't need to die in order to experience the underworld and heavens – those depths of consciousness and the heights of aware-ness. Humans have known this for centuries and have written, taught, and practiced this. For one example, the Kabbalah is *filled* with teachings and methods for making passage to and through the heavens. More on this in Chapter Four.

The following Cayce readings (5754-1 through -3) shed some fascinating light on the nature of sleep. Since the sleep state and the dreams that come from it are stimulated by our passage-in-consciousness practice it is helpful to study these readings. I have edited them for easier reading and clarity. Even so, they are particularly difficult readings, requiring our patience and concentrated attention. Read slowly. If you don't understand something, continue on. When you come across something that you do feel some understanding for, pause and reflect upon that.

"First, we would say, sleep is a shadow of that intermission in earth's experiences, that state called 'death'; for the physical consciousness becomes unaware of existent conditions — save for the attributes of those that partake of the imaginative or subconscious and unconscious forces of that same body.

"The sixth sense partakes of the *accompanying* entity that is ever on guard before the throne of the Creator itself. This sixth sense is that as may be known as the other self of the entity. There is a *definite* connection between that we have chosen to term the sixth sense and the other self within self.

"This sixth sense activity is the activating power or force of the other self. What other self? That which has been builded by the entity through its experiences as a whole in the material and cosmic world, see? It is a faculty of the soul-body itself. When the physical consciousness is at rest, the other self communes with the SOUL of the body, see? — correlating with that as the entity has accepted as its criterion or standard.

"Hence, we may find that an individual may from sorrow sleep and wake with a feeling of elation. What has taken place? Through such an association in sleep there may have come that peace, that understanding, through that passage of the selves in sleep. Hence we find the more spiritual-minded individuals are the more easily pacified, at peace, harmony, in normal active state as well as sleep. Why? They have set before themselves that that IS a criterion that may be wholly relied upon. For that from which an entity or soul sprang is its CONCEPT, its awareness of, the Divine or Creative Forces within their experience. Hence they that have named the Name of the Son have put their trust in Him. He is their standard, their model, their hope, their activity. Hence we see how the activity through such sleep, or such quieting as to enter the silence, is entering the presence of that which IS the criterion of the selves of an entity!

"On the other hand, oft we find one may retire with a feeling of elation, or peace, and awaken with a feeling of depression, of aloofness, of being alone, of being without hope, or of fear entering, and the body-physical awakes with that depression that manifests itself as of low spirits, as is termed, or of coldness, gooseflesh over the body [goose bumps?]. What has taken place? A comparison in that the poet has called the 'arms of Morpheus,' in that silence, in that relationship of the physical self to the soul. If one has set self in array against that of love as manifested by the Creator, then there MUST be a continual WARRING of those.

"By comparison we find that energy of creation manifested in the Son, such that one could say 'He sleeps,' while to the outward eye it was death; for He WAS - and IS - and ever will be - Life and Death in one. As we find ourselves in His presence in the sleep state, we then compare — have we builded in the soul that which makes for condemnation or that which is pleasing in His presence? So, my son, my daughter, let thine lights be in Him, for these are the MANNERS through which all may come to an understanding of the activities. As was given, 'I was in the Spirit on the Lord's day. I was caught up to the seventh heaven. Whether I was in the body or out of the body I cannot tell.' What was taking place? The subjugation of the physical attributes in accord and attunement with its infinite force as set as its ideal brought to that soul. Then came the response, 'Well done, thou good and faithful servant, enter into the joys of thy Lord. He that would be the greatest among you - not as the Gentiles, not as the heathen, not as the scribes or Pharisees, but - 'He that would be the greatest will be the SERVANT of all.'

"Which of these must be trained? The sixth sense? Or, must the body be trained in its other functionings to the dictates of the sixth sense?

"What, then, has this to do - you ask - with the subject of sleep? Sleep - that period when the soul takes stock of that it has acted upon during one rest period to another - making or drawing comparisons that make for Life itself in its ESSENCE. As harmony, peace, joy, love, long-suffering, patience brotherly love, kindness are the fruits of the Spirit. Hate, harsh words, unkind thoughts, oppressions and the like, are the fruits of the evil forces, or Satan. The soul either abhors that it has passed through, or enters into the joy of its Lord. This is an ESSENCE of that which is intuitive in the active forces. Why should this be so in sleep and not in wakefulness? How received woman her awareness? Through the sleep of the man! Hence INTUITION is an attribute of that portion of self brought to awareness by the suppression of those forces from which it sprang, yet self is endowed with all of those abilities and forces of its Maker.

"In a three dimensional world, a material world, beings must see a materialization to become aware of its existence in that plane, yet all are aware of the essence of Life itself, as the air that is breathed carries those elements that are not aware consciously of any existence to the body, yet the body lives upon such. In sleep all things become possible, as one finds self flying through space, lifting, or being chased, or what not, by those very things that make for a comparison of that which has been builded by the very soul of the body itself.

"Those who are nearer the spiritual realm, their visions, dreams and the like occur more often and are more often retained by the individual. For the first law is self-preservation. Thus self rarely desires to condemn self, except when the selves are warring one with another. If the ideal of the individual is lost, then the abilities to contact the spiritual forces are gradually lost or barriers are builded that prevent the individual from sensing of the nearness to a spiritual development.

"Whether the body desires it or not, in sleep the consciousness physically is laid aside. As to what will be or what will it seek depends upon what has been builded. What has it associated itself with, physically, mentally, spiritually? The closer the associations in the mental and physical with the spiritual, then - as has been seen by those attempting to produce a certain character of vision or dream - these follow the universal law: Like begets like! That which is sown in honor is reaped in glory. That which is sown in corruption cannot be reaped in glory. And, the likings are associations that are the comparisons of that which has been builded. Such experiences as dreams, visions and the like are but the ACTIVITIES in the unseen world of the real self of an entity.

"Ready for questions.

"Q: How may one train the sixth sense?

"A: That which is constantly associated in the mental visioning, in the imaginative forces, that which is constantly associated with the senses of the body, that will it develop towards. There are NO individuals who haven't at SOME TIME been warned as respecting that that may arise in their daily or physical experience! Do they heed? Do they heed to that as may be given as advice? No! Then, it must be experienced!

"Q: How may one be constantly guided by the accompanying entity on guard at the Throne?

"A: It is there! It's as to whether they desire it or not! It doesn't leave but is the active force. As to its ability to SENSE the variations in the experiences, it is as given in the illustration: 'As to whether in the body or out of the body, I cannot tell.' Hence this sense is the ability of the entity to associate to that realm it seeks for its associations during sleep periods, see?

"The subconscious and the abnormal, or the unconscious is the mind of the soul. That is, the sense that is used is of the subconscious or subliminal self that is on guard ever with the Throne itself. Has it not been said, 'He has given his angels charge concerning thee, lest at any time thou dashes thy foot against a stone.' Have you heeded? Then, He is near. Have you disregarded? Then, He has withdrawn to thine own self, see? That self that has been builded, that is as the comparison that must be presented - that IS presented - before the Throne itself! CONSCIOUSNESS - see - man seeks this for his OWN diversion. In sleep the soul seeks the REAL diversion, or the REAL activity of self.

"Q: What governs the experiences of the astral body while in the fourth dimensional plane during sleep?

"A: That upon which it has fed. That which it has builded. That which it seeks. That which the mental mind, the subconscious mind, the subliminal mind, SEEKS! That governs.

"Then, we come to an understanding of, 'He that would find must seek.' In the physical or material this we understand. That is a pattern of the subliminal or the spiritual self.

"Q: What state or trend of development is indicated if an individual does not remember dreams?

"A: The negligence of its associations, physically, mentally and spiritually.

"Q: Does one dream continually but simply fail to remember consciously?

"A: Continues an association or withdraws from that which IS its right, or its ability to associate! There is no difference in the unseen world to that that is visible, except in the unseen so much greater expanse or space may be covered! Does one always desire to associate itself with others? Do individuals always seek companionship? Do they withdraw themselves? That same desire carries on in the unseen world! See? It's a NATURAL experience! It's NOT an unnatural - it is nature - it is God's activity! His associations with man. His DESIRE to make for man a way for an understanding! Is there seen or understood fully that illustration that was given of the Son of man: that while those in the ship were afraid because of the elements [the storm], the Master of the sea slept. What associations may there have been with that sleep? Was it a natural withdrawing? Yet, when spoken to, the sea and the winds obeyed His voice. Thou may do even as He, wilt thou make thineself aware of the ability of those forces within self to communicate with, understand, those elements of the spiritual life IN the conscious and unconscious, these be one!

"Q: Is it possible for a conscious mind to dream while the astral or spirit body is absent?

"A: There may be dreams. It's as one's ability to divide self and do two things at once.

"The ability to read music and play is using different faculties of the same mind. Different portions of the same consciousness. Then, for one faculty to function while another is functioning in a different direction is not only possible but probable, dependent upon the ability of the individual to concentrate, or to centralize in their various places those functionings that are manifest of the spiritual forces in the material plane. BEAUTIFUL, isn't it?"

For our practical use, let's restate some of the key concepts and guidelines presented in these readings.
1. There are two selves, an outer self who usually loses consciousness during sleep and an inner self who gains consciousness during sleep. The outer self, the personality, is associated with the seen world. The

inner self, the soul-self, is associated with the unseen world.

2. The unseen world is no different than the seen except that in the unseen so much greater expanse or space may be experienced. The same desires, attitudes, and habits carry over into the unseen from the seen.

3. The inner self has a sixth sense. This sixth sense is the activating power or force of the inner self. The outer self must be trained to subjugate its influence to the control of the inner self in order for this power to fully manifest.

4. During sleep, a review and evaluation goes on, measuring the day's activities and thoughts against a standard or criterion. If the Son of God is the criterion, then one enters into that Presence and is either pleased or repelled by one's behavior.

5. The two selves can war with one another if the activities and thoughts of the outer self do not fit the goals and needs of the inner self, or do not measure up to the criterion held as the ideal.

6. The essence of life is ever present, even when not seen or consciously perceived. as air is to a physical body. The essence of real life is harmony, peace, joy, love, long-suffering, patience, brotherly love, and kindness. Hate, harsh words, greed, selfishness, unkind thoughts, oppressions and the like, pollute the air and slowly kill the real essence of life.

7. That which is intuitive in the outer life is the essence of the inner, real life. And, intuition is acquired by suppressing the outer's influence in order to allow the inner to surface, endowed with all those abilities and forces of its Maker. Thus, in sleep, when the outer is suppressed and the inner is active, all things become possible.

8. What one seeks, one finds. The inner self is ever ready to manifest, but it must be sought, desired.

9. What one feeds upon physically, mentally and emotionally, one attracts when entering into the unseen world of sleep.

10. It is a NATURAL experience.

Dream Recall & Interpretation

Now that we have some idea of the dynamics of dreaming and the development of the sixth sense, let's look at Cayce's tips for dream recall.

First, since slipping into asleep is actually a transition from conscious mind to subconscious, and since the subconscious is so amendable to suggestion, Cayce recommends that we give ourselves a pre-sleep suggestion (as we are falling asleep) to recall our dreams.

Second, since the conscious mind is not having the dream and is in control of the central nervous system (which operates much of the movement of the body), Cayce recommends that we not move the body immediately upon awakening. Rather, lie still and scan your deeper mind for the dream content.

Finally, once the content is present, transfer it over to the conscious mind and write it down in a dream journal. Much will be gained by your dream study. Think of it as going to college, the college of the soul and spirit. Graduation is fully knowing yourself to be your true and complete self, and yet one with the Whole. Within us is the greatest teacher of all.

Tips for Remembering & Understanding

Pre-sleep suggestion: As we fall asleep we are moving from the conscious mind to the subconscious, dreaming mind. The subconscious is amenable to suggestion. Therefore, give it a suggestion to remember your dreams. One suggestion that is used in the Cayce organization is: "Now I'm going to sleep deeply and will wake feeling refreshed, revitalized, and remembering my dreams."

Don't move the body upon waking: To move the physical body requires the conscious mind. Since it is not the dreaming mind, we do not want to engage it too quickly in the morning, allowing the subconscious to give its content to the conscious mind gradually and completely. Lie still for this important transfer of data.

Get the gist of it first, details second: Feel the essence of the dream's meaning first, and don't let the details sway you from the fundamental essence or spirit of the dream.

Use the essence of the dream in life: Knowledge not applied is lost and becomes a stumbling block rather than a steppingstone.

Keep a journal, but keep it simple: Dream themes are developed over a series of dreams. Inner processing takes several dreams. Detailed guidance takes several dreams. Write them down. Read over them. But don't let it become a burden. Keep it a dynamic, changing part of real life. The inner and outer are a team.

Tips for Interpreting Dreams

Here's a good sequence of steps to help us correctly interpret a dream:

Identify the MOOD: up, down, or neutral; scared or daring, sad or happy, worried or hopeful, and so on. Mood reveals our inner-self's fundamental feelings.

Identify the SUBJECT. Refine this to the lowest common denominator: What is the subject that is being viewed? Not the action. Not the feeling. The subject. The matter under consideration.

Identify the MOVEMENT: watching, listening, waiting, reflecting, and the like; or doing, acting, changing, making, running toward, and the like; or protecting, warning, retreating, running away, and the like. Movement reveals our inner self's basic call to action, further reflection, or retreat.

Identify the NATURE of the inner mind's condition or disposition. Is it: reviewing, previewing, analyzing, processing, instructing, warning, encouraging, or experiencing? Determining the fundamental nature of the inner mind's activity helps us understand how to use the dream. In some cases, the dream is an experiencing, a processing, a reflecting, and calls for no action. In other cases, the dream is instructing, warning, or encouraging us, and action is called for.

The last two may seem very similar, and they are in some ways, but I've separated them because it helps me to think of "movement" as the action called for in the dream, while "nature" is the condition or disposition of the inner mind during the dream.

Let's review: As you wake, take note of the overall mood, then the subject, then the movement, and finally the nature of the mind while in the dream. Remember, it is best to do this while still in or near the dreaming mind because it is the best interpreter of the dream. Cayce always said that the dreamer was the best interpreter of the dream. And the dreamer is not our outer, intellectual selves but our inner, dreaming selves. Get the interpretation before you come completely out of the dreaming mind.

The Dream Stele between the paws of the Great
Sphinx tells the story of Prince Tuthmosis who falls
asleep near the Sphinx and dreamed that the Sphinx
promised him the throne of Egypt in return for
Tuthmosis clearing the sand away from around it.
Tuthmosis did as he was instructed in the dream and,
as promised in the dream, eventually became
Pharaoh Tuthmosis IV.

*Our minds attempt to live in the
stew of our bodies! Improve the ingredients
and you improve consciousness.*

Chapter 4
CONSCIOUSNESS & THE BODY

While we are practicing the passage in consciousness method and working with our dreams, we may wish to better understand how consciousness and the physical body interact, and how we may help bring cooperation between these two most important aspects of our being.

By "consciousness" I mean feelings, emotions, attitudes, thoughts, perceptions, prejudices, beliefs, fears, doubts, uncertainties, desires, urges, fantasies, dreams, nightmares, flashes of imagery, and so on – all the things that make up our mind and mental processes. And by "physical body" I mostly mean our two nervous systems: 1. *the central, cerebrospinal system* which is the complex of nerves that control the activities of the body – in we vertebrates it comprises our brain and spinal cord; and 2. *the autonomic system*: this is the part responsible for control of the bodily functions that are *not* consciously directed, such as breathing, the heartbeat, and digestive processes. The autonomic nervous system is composed of two parts: the *sympathetic nervous system* — designed to sympathetically *react* immediately to external and internal stimulus; and the *parasympathetic nervous system* — which *counterbalances* the actions of the sympathetic nerves, restoring the body to normalcy after dynamic sympathetic responses. The autonomic nervous system also consists of nerves arising from the brain and the lower end of the spinal cord and supplying the internal organs, blood vessels, and glands. Among the glands are the *endocrine* glands that affect the body through the blood system using *hormones*. Hormones are powerful "signaling" molecules that are transported through the circulatory system targeting organs to regulate physiology and behavior. *Behavior?* Yes, behavior, and here's one of the many connections between the consciousness and the physical body. And this is where ancient teachings about chakras, or metaphysical centers, within our bodies are affected by and affect the chemistry of our bodies, and in turn our behavior and consciousness. These endocrines glands are the physical vehicles of the metaphysical centers within us.

Here is Edgar Cayce's perspective on this in reading 281-38: "The glandular forces then are ever akin to the sources from which, through which, *the soul dwells within the body.*" And he expands on this, saying, "It may be easily seen, then, how very closely

78

the glands are associated with reproduction, degeneration, regeneration; and this throughout—not only the physical forces of the body but the mental body and the soul body." Here again we see the connection between the mental and physical, and how glandular secretion of hormones affect us, mentally and physically.

Now we can see how a good meditation practice, which passage-in-consciousness is, can improve our bodies and expand our minds. Chakras and lotuses of the Yoga Sutras are, according to Cayce, functioning through the glandular, hormonal system within us. And as many of us know, hormones affect our feelings. Here's a good example:

Let's consider one of the most powerful dynamics of human life, *love*. From a *hormonal* perspective love goes like this: Evolution's unswerving drive for survival of the species has developed a human body that is loaded with powerful chemicals to help ensure the success of human bonding. The "love chemical" is *phenylethylamine* (PEA). When this is released in the brain of *any* human, he or she will feel uncontrollably amorous, romantic, and "turned on" by the person who is the object of these feelings. Follow this up with a little *oxytocin* (often called "the cuddle chemical"), and you have the lovemaking sensations of relaxed satisfaction and attachment. For the relationship to endure, however, *endorphins* must be released in the brain. If they are, then the love relationship endures. And you thought it was just destiny or opportunity! It likely was but for love to truly work, it must work through the body. And that is exactly how the soul and mind through the glands influence the body and the body influences the soul and mind using the body. Image if we could affect what hormones were being released and when. This would be significant. In the next chapter we'll learn how to raise the vibrations of our body and in turn affect the nature and timing of hormonal influences. But let's locate these major glands in the human body.

In the following illustrations you'll see where these glands are in our bodies. Note: the Cells of Leydig (named after the doctor that discovered them) are in and around gonads but correlate with Yoga's navel chakra. The root chakra correlates to the reproductive glands (as an ovary or testis) that produces gametes. A gamete is a mature haploid (a single set of unpaired chromosomes) male or female germ cell that is able to unite with another to form a zygote (a cell that is formed when an egg and a sperm combine). But for our meditative purposes, the root chakra is a life-creating dynamic within our human bodies, and may be enlivened and raised up through the spinal column to enliven the whole body, and in turn positively affect consciousness.

From here we move to the solar plexus chakra of our bodies, which is just below our rib cage and sternum, in the center of the torso, and is associated with the adrenal glands on top of our kidneys, as well as the pancreas.

Then we move to the heart chakra which is not the pump but the gland known as the thymus, and became famous due to HIV/AIDS and the T-cells. A T-cell, along with a CD4 cell, is a lymphocyte which actively participates in the immune response by fighting infections.

From here we move to the throat chakra, which relates to the thyroid gland, one of the largest glands in the body. The thyroid gland controls how quickly the body uses energy, makes proteins, and controls the body's sensitivity to other hormones. It stores and produces hormones that affect the function of virtually every organ in our bodies. It is also associated with modest changes in body weight and energy levels.

Finally we move into the brain and the two major glands: the pineal and the pituitary. The pineal gland secrets melatonin, which affects the cycles of sleep and wakefulness. How we think and feel every day depends on the pineal gland. The pituitary gland is often dubbed the "master gland" because its hormones control other parts of the endocrine system.

In the following illustrations we see the location of these glands in the human body and some of the pathways and techniques related to enlightenment.

Explanation of the Temple to Body

Using the illustrations page 84, Let's go through the Luxor Temple in Egypt correlating its various chambers with "chambers" in our physical bodies.

See the "Colonnaded Courtyard" #11 in both the lower and up images? That correlates to our abdominal cavity (our belly, with navel and solar plexus chakras). Now look for the Hypostyle Hall #24. That correlates to our rib cage and heart chakra (thymus gland). "Hypostyle" is a pillared hall and the pillars symbolize our ribs. Now look for #25, a narrow passageway leading into the holier areas of the temple. This narrow passage is our throat and throat chakra, which is the thyroid gland. This passageway is not shown in the small temple illustration, just the overview. Next look for the "Barque" (Boat) chamber #15 in both the lower and up images. This is the awakening of the mind, for the boat or "barque" of the godlings is used to sail across the river of fantasy and thoughts to higher levels of consciousness. Right after this is the Sanctuary in two parts: the "Holy Place," #19, and then the Holy of Holies, #18 in the illustration. The "Holy Place" in Cayce's view is the pineal gland in the center of our brain. The pituitary gland, the master gland of the human body, is the "Holy of Holies."

The Holy of Holies is the highest level in this stone temple, which is built on a slop from the entrance rising to the Holy of Holies. When in the Sanctuary one can look back and see the entire pathway leading through the temple, correlating with the human body from lower chakras to higher. The journey is an external ritual of an internal process that leads from ordinary, daily energy and consciousness up through transitions to higher energy and vibes with a raised and expanded consciousness. Wonderful, isn't it? I've walked this temple roughly 35 times. I can imagine the initiations and ceremonies that once occurred here – with processions of white-robed and gold-adorned initiates led by priests and priestesses. Now, today, it is for us to make this journey WITHIN ourselves. And from my experience practicing and teaching meditation for many year it is truly a challenge for a predominately 3D physical person raised in this outer world and its reality to go within themselves to some sanctuary of higher vibes and consciousness. Back in the 1960s we were all in touch with vibrations as evidenced by the hit song "Good Vibrations" by the Beach Boys. But life has a way of capturing all of our attention, and time has a way of challenging our efforts to budget regular time for raising vibes and consciousness.

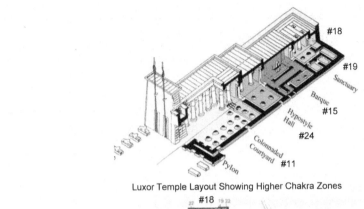

Luxor Temple Layout Showing Higher Chakra Zones

Illustration Credit: Brown Univ. & Carol Meyer

The Luxor Temple arranged as an *outer* depiction of the pathways and chambers *within* the human body, which is the ultimate temple (explained on pp. 82-83).

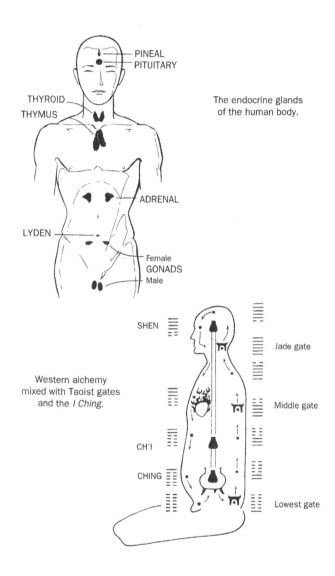

The Endocrine glands correlating to chakras within the human body temple. The lower image reveals the life energy and its alchemical power when circulated.

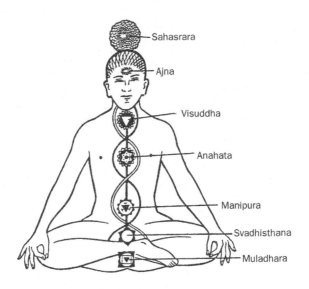

The Chakra System.

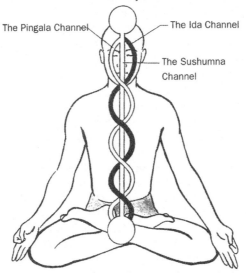

The three channels of the kundalini energy.

From the *Yoga Sutras* by Patanjali

Conceiving and nourishing the spirit-body
in the womb of consciousness
during meditation (from the taoist text
The Secret of the Golden Flower).

Meditation, Stage 3: Separation of the spirit-body for independent existence.

1000	*Ho Nikōn,* "The Conqueror"
999	*Epistēmōn,* Intuitively Wise
888	*Iēsous,* the Higher Mind
	I. "The Lamb"
777	*Stauros,* the Cross
666	*Hē Phrēn,* the Lower Mind
	II. "The Beast"
555	*Epithumia,* Desire
	III. "The Red Dragon"
444	*Spirēma,* the Serpent-coil
333	*Akrasia,* Sensuality
	IV. "The False Seer"

The Gnostic Chart Concealed in the Apocalypse

A Gnostic chart that combines concepts from
the Cabala, the Revelation, and the chakra system.

Secret teachings in ancient schools.

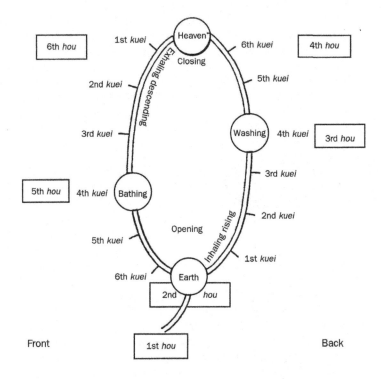

The circulation of the light from the taoist text *The Secret of the Golden Flower*. Note how the energy is drawn up the body with inhalation and then moved down the body with exhalation. Getting the energy moving is the goal. The light results naturally from the circulation process.

This diagram reveals the Taoist teaching about correlating the circulation of the breath with the circulation of bodily energy to raise the level and vibration of the body's life force (kundalini).

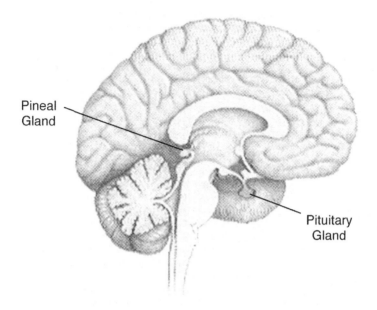

Pineal
Gland

Pituitary
Gland

The two highest endocrine glands in the human body
are the pineal and the pituitary, correlating to the two
highest spiritual centers or chakras in the body temple.
Notice the spinal cord descending from the brain into
the spinal column – this is how the cranial nerves and
spinal nerve roots communicate and protect themselves
immunologically. The vagus nerve, historically cited as
the *pneumogastric* nerve, is the tenth *cranial* nerve, and
it interfaces with parasympathetic control of the heart
and digestive tract. Besides providing output to various
organs, the vagus nerve comprises between 80% and
90% of afferent nerves (those carrying messages to the
brain), and is mostly conveying *sensory* information
about the state of the body's organs to the central
nervous system. Metaphysically, this is a major pathway
of the life force and subliminal consciousness within the
body temple during meditation.

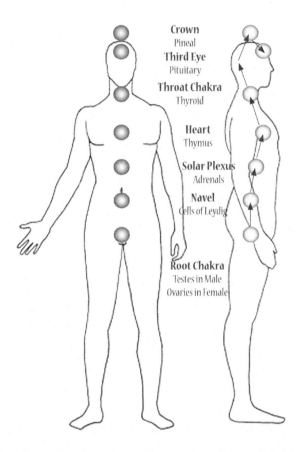

Crown
Pineal
Third Eye
Pituitary
Throat Chakra
Thyroid
Heart
Thymus
Solar Plexus
Adrenals
Navel
Cells of Leydig
Root Chakra
Testes in Male
Ovaries in Female

This illustration shows the ancient flow of the kundalini (the life force) within the body during meditative practices. Notice that it is the form of a cobra in the attack position. Cayce concurs with this pattern rather than the common one which teaches that the energy goes straight up to the crown of the head. Rather, it goes to the base of the brain, then the center of the brain, and then over to the forehead and large frontal lobe of the human brain - as depicted on Tut's golden mask.

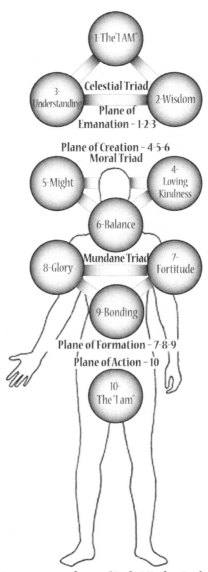

Interconnectedness of Body, Mind, & Soul with Orbs
The Tree of Life and the Planes of Existence are
interconnected in our being: body, mind, and soul.

This image reveals the classic Kabbalah emanations,
triads, and planes of consciousness.

The Kabbalah illustration on the previous page (91) is from my book on the Kabbalah (see a list of my books on page 184). The illustration depicts the Kabbalah Tree of Life emanations of God superimposed over the human body temple. It also shows the 3 great Triads: Celestial, Moral, and Mundane, correlating to the Infinite Awareness, Guiding Conscience Awareness, and Earthly/Personal Awareness. The Celestial is above the carnal body in the expanded of higher vibes and consciousness. The Moral is in the large frontal lobe of the human, which so distinguishes a human brain from all animal brains. And the Mundane is consciousness that most humans function in throughout daily life.

The illustration also shows the 4 major planes of life: 1. The plane of Emanation, from which we were first conceived and given independent consciousness; 2. The plane of Consciousness, in which we have our higher mind and the gift of free-will; 3. The plane of Formation, in which we began to move from pure spirit or pure energy into thought-forms and eventually into matter; and 4. The plane of Action, in which the stage is set, the characters assembled, and the karmic scripts are played out as one of Shakespeare's plays, with drama, tragedy, comedy, and hopefully resolution of the dilemma: thesis, antithesis, and synthesis! In spite of the apparent elements and stages and planes, there is an unbreakable oneness that needs to be discovered, as it is seen in how the 1st and 10th emanation are the "I AM" of the Creator and the "I am" of created.

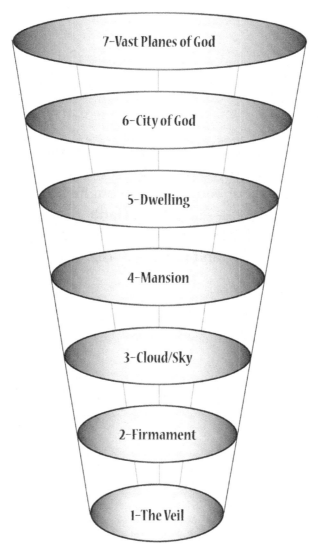

The Kabbalah Seven Levels of Heaven correlating to seven levels of consciousness.

"Breath is the bridge which connects
life to consciousness, which unites
your body to your thoughts."
–Thich Nhat Hanh
(Buddhist monk, teacher, author, poet,
and peace activist)

Chapter 5
RAISING OUR VIBRATIONS

Throughout ancient cultures and mystical teachings there were three methods for raising the vibrations of the human body: breathing, chanting, and imaginative mind movement.

Breathing methods for raising vibrations are many but we'll look at two, one from Edgar Cayce's files and one from Taoism as described in the book *The Secret of the Golden Flower: A Chinese Book of Life*, translated by Richard Wilhelm with a commentary by Dr. Carl Jung (London 1931).

The Circulation Breath (See illustration on page 88.)

In this Taoist text the master teacher Liu Huayang wrote: "There is a turn upward toward Heaven when the breath is drawn in. When the breath flows out, energy is directed towards the Earth. In two intervals one gathers Sacred Energy." He describes a breathing method that blends life essence of higher consciousness with earthly, bodily forces — resulting in illuminating levels of awareness and greater bodily health. He explains that *circulating* the breath is better than just pumping it or maximizing breaths so as to affect the condition of the oxygen in the blood. Here's how it is done, and it is quite simple.

It is described as the circulation Consciousness and Life, and goes like this: Breathe through your nostrils in a normal manner; however, with each inhalation *feel and imagine* the life force being drawn up from the pelvic and lower tummy parts of your body to the crown of your head and over to the third-eye center on your brow. Hold the breath slightly, and sense the *union of the finite with the infinite,* of the yin with the yang. Then, as you exhale, feel and imagine the Consciousness and Life Force *bathing the chakras* as it descends through each to the lowest center (root and navel chakras). Pause in the empty breath. Then inhale while again feeling and imagining the drawing upward of the Life Force from lower to higher regions of the body temple. Repeat these breathing cycles at a comfortable pace — using your consciousness (imagination and visualization) and your breath to move the Life Force with each inhalation and exhalation.

As the breath and life force *rise,* feel and imagine how they enliven the energy centers of your body and move that energy to higher levels. And at the same time notice how this awakens and opens the lotuses of your consciousness. As breath and life force *descend*, feel how they *bathe* the body temple.

Take your time; again, consider this as an integral part of the meditation process. Do about seven to twelve cycles of inhalations and exhalations – *slowly* and attentively. Be fully aware of what you are doing.

Cayce's Polarity Breath

He is Cayce's premeditation breathing method: Deeply inhale through your *right* nostril by pressing your left nostril closed with your finger, filling your lungs, and feeling *strength* throughout your body as you inhale. Hold the breath for a moment. Then, exhale slowly and completely *through your mouth*. Pause with empty lungs for a moment. This empty-breath pause is a good place to feel silence and stillness. Then again, repeat the inhalation through the right nostril, filling the lungs, and *feeling strength*. Do three of these right-nostril breaths. Next, inhale through the *left* nostril while feeling yourself opening to the Source of Life (pressing your right nostril closed with your finger while inhaling). Hold the breath for a moment, then exhale slowly through the *right nostril not the mouth*, by pressing your left nostril closed with your finger. Pause with empty lungs for a moment. This empty-breath pause is a good place to feel the Life Force in and above your head. Do this breath three times.

During the first part of this breathing exercise (inhaling through the right nostril and exhaling through the mouth) you should feel *strength*. During the second part (inhaling through the left nostril and exhaling through the right nostril) you should feel *uplifting and opening of the spiritual forces* of the body. If possible it is good to have fresh air in the room while doing this breathing exercise, to bring more oxygen into the circulatory system and brain.

Edgar Cayce Readings on
Raising Consciousness and Vibrations.

"(Q) How may I bring into activity my pineal and pituitary glands, as well as the Kundalini and other chakras, that I may attain to higher mental and spiritual powers? Are there exercises for this purpose, and if there are, please give them.

"(A) As indicated, first so FILL the mind with the ideal that it may vibrate throughout the whole of the MENTAL being!

"Then, close the desires of the fleshly self to conditions about same. MEDITATE upon 'THY WILL WITH ME.' Feel same. Fill ALL the centers of the body, from the lowest to the highest, with that ideal; opening the centers by surrounding self first with that consciousness, 'NOT MY WILL BUT THINE, O LORD, BE DONE IN AND THROUGH ME.'

"And then, have that desire, that purpose, not of attaining without HIS direction, but WITH His direction – who is the Maker, the Giver of life and light; as it is indeed in Him that we live and move and have our being.

"(Q) Is there any method whereby I might develop such faculties as a perfect memory; intuition, telepathy, astral projection, and healing of others, as well as myself?

"(A) All healing of every nature comes from the DIVINE within that body, or the body applied to such methods or manners of healing.

"The attuning of self – not as to that this or that may be accomplished. But remember, as has ever been given of old, ALL manner of expression, all life, emanates from one source - God! God in thyself; not as 'I will, but as Thou wilt.'

"Let that be the purpose, the import, the intent, the DESIRE; and that which is needed for the bringing of its abilities and faculties of every nature in attunement will be done.

"And thus give off, in harmonious accent, that as will be pleasing in His sight – the purpose for which each soul enters a material experience.

(Q) "How may I best be used as a channel to be of mental and spiritual assistance to others?

"(A) First by finding self and self's relationship with the Creative Forces [that are] being manifested in thy daily activity, thy daily speech, thy daily conversation, thy daily convocation with thy fellow men – that each activity is as unto the Lord!" (1861-4)

"(Q) Please give a discourse on each of the seven major glandular centers, as I call them, that will help us and others to have a better understanding of their functions physically and mentally during the adolescent period, the adult period and the changing period; also mentally and spiritually during meditation, opening of the door, the baptism of the Holy Spirit....

(A) "We should begin with the *first cause*, if an understanding is to be maintained! These pass along the way that has to do with the *co-relating* of physical, mental, and spiritual understanding." (281-58)

"(Q) As the life force passes through the glands it illuminates them.

"(A) In meditation, yes. In the life growth, yes and no." (281-53)

"(Q) Please give advice that would help in those times when there is the beginning of Kundalini to rise or there is the circulation of Kundalini through the body. What should be the next step?

"(A) Surround self with that consciousness of the Christ-Spirit; this by the affirmation of "Let self be surrounded with the Christ-Consciousness, and the DIRECTIONS be through those activities in the body-force itself. Do not seek the lower influences, but the Christ-Consciousness. " (2072-11)

"(Q) What can be done to clear up the congestion in the fluid inside the spine, called by some the kundalini? Will yoga breaths aid?

"(A) As we find, rather the influences of the *massage* will alleviate the pressures on those centers along the spine from which impulses are received to the superficial circulation from the deeper cerebrospinal impulses, and would bring the better assimilated forces in the glandular activity.

"Yoga breathing has its place, but when a condition has reached the place where there is the lack of the forces that PRODUCE same – then supply them by release in the system of those centers from which impulse may be had." (1703-2)

"(Q) Is there a physical reason, such as congested Kundalini, curved spine, or loosely connected etheric body, or any karmic reason, for my not hearing The Voice of the Silence or getting SELF-Realization?

"(A) Only within self. For He has promised. He will speak if you tune in.

"(Q) How can I overcome it? [He's referring to bodily problems with higher vibrations resulting from meditation methods that raise the life force (kundalini) in his body.]

"(A) In thine own consciousness. Walk with, talk with, Him." (1703-3) In many of Cayce's readings the "Him" referred to was the Father, the Creator as the Creative Forces and the Universal Consciousness.

"(Q) Through my meditation, has the kundalini fire risen to the head or top of spine at base of skull? If so, was it because of sex abstinence and discipline that this happened?

"(A) It has risen at TIMES, but has not remained; else there would NOT be those periods of confusion. For, when this has arisen and is disseminated properly through the seven centers of the body, it has purified the body from all desire of sex relationships. For, THIS IS an outlet through which one may attain to celibacy. That it has NOT REMAINED indicates changes." (2329-1) Let's keep in mind that Cayce's readings were not uncomfortable with human sexual activity, in face, they stated that such would be the natural result of two people growing closer with one another in the spirit of caring, of loving. In this reading he was simply affirming that if one wanted or needed to be celibate, then meditation was an outlet for the sexual energy. And this by raising the energy from the lower chakras to the higher ones. From Cayce's perspective sexual energy is simply the life force manifesting in sexuality, and the life force may manifest in other outlets, such as creativity, life-giving healing, life-channeled hard work, and the like.

This same person got a follow-up reading (numbered 2329-2) in which Cayce said this:

"In the nervous system we find *physically*, or pathologically, some effects of the raising of the kundalini, or the imaginative system, to the reactions along the centers of the cerebrospinal system, without their *sources* being *gratified*. This produces oft those effects of the exhaustions to the body, and at such times the assimilating and digestive systems are disturbed. Not that there are *mental* reactions of a detrimental nature, but mental reactions of complex natures naturally are the results. These as we find are much of the sources of the nervous tensions. Not that these — the raising of such forces — should not be accomplished in a body; but their sources, their reactions must of necessity find expression.

"For this body we find that these may find the greater expression [outlet] in just aiding, helping, someone not so fortunate as self – in the mental, the spiritual, and the physical balance.

However, there will be necessitated a supplying to the system of those sources of energies that have been expended in these activities; and thus we may replenish and rebuild the better reactions, as well as maintain a better physical functioning of the organs of the system. For, naturally, with the vital energies and vital nerve forces used or expended, there is a weakening to the vital activities of heart, liver, and kidneys. Not that these are involved organically, save sympathetic reaction in the present. In the organs brain forces and the imaginative forces, the sensory reactions, are very good; though there are times when the body becomes rather supersensitive. This finds reaction through the organs of the sensory or sympathetic nervous system. These, too, will be materially aided with the addition, or the supplying to the body in the most natural means, of those energies and vital forces to keep the body better physically fit.

"The using of these energies has caused not organic but SYMPATHETIC, functional reactions to heart, to liver, to kidneys. These find expression in that when one becomes overactive there is the natural reaction in the opposite direction to the other, in most instances. While not as yet vital disturbances, there *are* those inclinations that may be materially aided in the present.

"We would begin first with the physiotherapy treatments of a *general* hydrotherapy and massage nature; not just a massage as from a masseuse, but the general hydrotherapy treatments in which there is a stimulation to the superficial circulation. These would include, then, those applications of both heat and cold – either in the plain bath ... or in the cold and hot water, especially *directly* to the spine and to these areas of the body. Then follow these with the thorough rubdown with stimulating oils, as well as the rubs to close the pores after such [note: heat opens the pores, and cold closes them].

"There should be required thirty to forty to fifty minutes, or more, for these applications; at least once a week, until eight to ten to twelve such applications are taken. After the first four or five such hydrotherapy treatments, we would then begin with ... the balance of the vitamin forces, the reactions of the iron as well as the glandular forces for better stimulations to the energies used, will not only prevent colds or congestion but will aid in keeping a balance for this body. Keep these up for at least six to eight weeks; and we should find a great improvement.

"And with the change in the physical attitudes, and the activity giving an outlet to the energies through expending them in helpful forces for some less fortunate, we find that the mental, the spiritual, and physical will be brought to a closer coordination."

The individual got a third reading about maintaining emotional stability when bodily vibes and mental consciousness is raised and yet one has to live in the material world with other more earthly focused people.

"(Q) How may I bring about greater emotional stability?

"(A) As the body-mind entertains and enters into the raising of the kundalini influence through the body, surround self with the light of the Christ-

Consciousness by thought, by word of mouth, by impressing it upon self. And in that light there may be never any harm to self or to the emotions of the body, or any fear of the mental and spiritual self being entertained or used by the dark influence." (2329-3)

In this next reading Cayce actually connects illness to the raising of the life force (kundalini) when the body is in good condition.

2334-1

"This [practice] at times gives a great deal of anxiety partially is due to the reflexes from the high vibratory forces to which the body may raise itself by the concentration and meditation; which, causing the kundalini to rise along the cerebrospinal system, or in conjunction with the pineal, gives to the lower portion of the pelvis and the abdomen – under certain stresses – a great deal of disturbance.

"The body physically should never attempt to use, or to concentrate on raising this activity of the spiritual and mental forces, when over hungry, or *never* just after eating; for these tend to cause (that is, the concentration and meditation) other portions of the system to become rather subject to, or subjugated, or stopped, during such periods. When there is undernourishment it causes a flow ... as to form the same character as adhering particles through the system. When there is an oversupply or digestion is not completed, it causes an engorging in the lower portion of the caecum; thus adding to or forming those forces in that area where prolapses has been indicated.

"These taxations then cause also disturbances to the sensory system.

"Hence this heaviness at times across the small of the back, again that about the middle of the back and at the base of the brain; those reflexes or incoordinations between the cerebrospinal and sympathetic or vegetative or sensory system. They're out of accord. These have caused some disturbance to the sensory system, as well as the general debilitation as indicated with the eyes, the ears, at times the taste. All of these become *supersensitive* at times, and at others suffer from the effect of *over stress*. This is especially indicated in the eyes.

"In making for corrective forces, all of these influences should be taken into consideration; first those things indicated regarding activities of the mental and spiritual forces under physical disturbance – either lack of food or oversupply of same, see, or digestion not completed.

"Then, the character, the quality and quantity of the foods should be considered. For this body, we would give this as a general outline; though, to be sure, this does not indicate ALL the foods that are to be taken, merely a general outline:

"Mornings – either citrus fruits with whole wheat toast, coffee, tea or milk, OR a cooked cereal. But do not have the cereal AND the citrus fruit at the same meal; and when the cereal is used, choose those of the nature – both cooked and dry – that carry the extra vitamins B and B-1 and G; that will supply the blood forces as well as to aid in the phosphorous and iron as indicated in G and A. These, then, are necessary elements, and the morning is a good period for the assimilation of same, after the period of rest.

"Noons – a little fish, fowl or lamb, but never any foods fried. Have raw vegetables as combined with some soup, or fruit juices, or stews. Never take any red meat of any kind.

"Evenings – principally vegetables; especially onions, leeks, beans, and such natures – preferably the green beans, not too much of any that are of the dried variety. The yam and the squash, especially the yellow – never the white – all of these should be a part of the evening meal, as part of the diet; for these also, in an easily assimilated manner, carry those elements needed.

Plenty of fruits, cooked and raw, at all times – morning, noon, or night. Stewed fruits – as apricots, figs and such – all of these natures are well to be taken at either of the meals, but be mindful of the combinations that would conflict; that is, beware of the *acid-producing* foods that do not combine so much with the starches, for the acid fruits then become acid-producing when they should be alkaline-producing through the system.

"At least twice a month have a thorough massage, preferably the movements of the Swedish massage.

"In reference to the feet and the callous places – we would massage these places night and morning with a mixture of a tablespoonful of Castor Oil and a quarter teaspoonful of baking soda. Mix these ingredients thoroughly together and massage. Of course, this whole quantity would not be used all at once, unless necessary. After the massaging is completed, if necessary sponge off any excess in those areas. This will bring better forces for this body.

"Doing these, we find we will bring the better conditions for this body." (2334-1)

Here's another reading about meditating with incense and chanting.

"(Q) Please give instructions on meditation.

"(A) For this body - not for everybody - odors would have much to do with the ability of the entity to meditate. For, the entity in the experiences through the Temple of Sacrifice became greatly attuned through the sense of smell, for the activities were upon the olfactory nerves and muscles of the body itself. For there the protuberances were taken away.

"As to the manner of meditation, then: Begin with that which is oriental in its nature - oriental incense.

Let the mind become, as it were, attuned to such by the humming, producing those sounds of o-o-o-ah-ah-umm-o-o-o; not as to become monotonous, but *feel* the essence of the incense through the body-forces in its motion of body. This will open the kundalini forces of the body. Then direct same to be a blessing to others. These arise from the creative center of the body itself, and as they go through the various centers *direct same*; else they may become greater disturbing than helpful. Surround self ever with that purpose, 'Not my will, O God, but Thine be done, ever,' and the entity will gain vision, perception and - most of all - judgment." (2823-3)

Chanting

The body is uniquely designed for enhancing energy with sound because it has three primary sound chambers: the abdominal chamber in the lower torso (abdomen), the cardiopulmonary chamber of the chest, and the cranial chamber of the skull. Sound can be directed into these chambers and the resonance of chants changes the vibrations of atoms in cells and organs. These sounds also affect the mind-body connection, raising consciousness throughout the nervous system. Some chants use the voice and breath to vibrate select sounds in these three chambers.

Edgar Cayce gave chants that tune us to the Universal Consciousness. He gave several chants and even some insights into how chanting was used in ancient temples – particularly in an ancient Egyptian temple known as The Temple Beautiful.

Cayce said to use an incantation or chant that "carries self deeper - deeper - to the seeing, feeling, experiencing of that image in the creative forces of love, entering into the Holy of Holies within our brain and mind that inhabits it [see illustration on page 84]. As self feels or experiences the raising of this, see it disseminated through the inner eye [the mind's eye] to that which will bring the greater understanding in meeting every condition in the experience of the body. Then, listen to the music that is made as each center of your own body responds to that new creative force...."

Cayce's chanting is God-centered, meaning that it seeks to tune the chanter to the Divine Source of Life. He taught that such attunement naturally results in greater health, happiness, well-being, and enlightenment. Good chanting is *inner sounding*, not singing.

These chants begin by sounding first in the lower portions of the body – the root, navel, and solar plexus chakras – then the sounding shifts to higher portions of the body – the heart, throat – and then finally in the brain, stimulating the crown and forehead chakras [third eye]. But the chants are not just attempting to raise and transform bodily vibrations. Each chant attempts to lift and carry the mind and spirit to higher, more harmonic levels of attunement to the Divine Oneness (See Chapter 8).

Usually, the first series of chants are devoted to raising the vibrations of the body. For example, when chanting Cayce's *ar-ee-oo-mm* chant, the *ar* sounds are directed into the abdominal chamber and the lower chakras and the mind puts its attention in the area of the root and navel chakras – like this: ar-ar-rrr. Next the sound changes to the *ee*, one directs the vibrations of the voice to the upper portion of the abdominal chamber to the solar plexus area in the center of the torso, like this: *eeee*. Then, as we shift to the *oo* sounds we move our minds and vocal vibrations are directed to the heart chakra in the cardiopulmonary chamber and to the throat chakra, where the voice box is, like this: *ooooo* (a more advanced sounding of this is like a drawn out expression of pain in the English word *ow* – ooowww, leading directly into the *uuummm* sound (the *uuu* are *oo* as in *who*), holding the *mmmm* sound on the pineal and pituitary glands and chakras.

In order for you to complete an effective chant, you will need to take a deep breath and skilled control of your diaphragm. Actually, you will need to take *three-level* breath. Let me explain: In order to fill your lungs, you need to begin taking a breath in your *lower lungs* near your diaphragm, by expanding your belly, then inhale further by expanding your chest, and then still further by lifting your shoulders as you inhale, filling what feels like your upper back (the top of your lungs). Now your lungs are full. As you sound the chant, control the release of your breath by controlling your diaphragm – gradually passing the breath through your vocal cords. Practice this and you'll be able to do a good, long chant that will get you high and some good vibrations.

An often overlooked but a very important part of chanting is the *silence* that follows the *sounding*. Use this silence to feel, imagine, and know that your body, mind, and soul are rising to higher levels or deeper places of attunement. Ultimately, chanting leads to the deep silence of oneness with the central, indivisible Source of Life. There you abide silently as you are imbued with health, wellbeing, and enlightenment.

Find a regular place and a special time to enjoy the benefits of chanting. It won't require anything fancy or much time. All you need is your voice and good, clear intentions.

Now back to Cayce's readings on meditation:

"(Q) What is the condition of the Kundalini now, which was mentioned in my first reading?

"(A) This depends upon how and in what manner the body attempts to raise same during its meditation. This doesn't change, for it is the seat, or the source of life-giving forces in the body. The effect upon the body depends upon the use to which an individual entity puts same. Thus the warning as to how and for what such influences are raised within the body itself." (3481-3)

"These are the three centers through which there is activity of the kundalini forces that act as suggestions to the spiritual forces for distribution through the seven centers of the body." (3676-1) Cayce identified these three as the third cervical plexus, the ninth "dorsal" or thoracic plexus, and the fourth lumbar plexus.

"We find that the entity should find its spiritual ideal - and not in the mysteries of the East. Not that these haven't their place in the experiences of individuals, but the abilities of this entity in the earthly sojourns have been such that unless there is the *whole* Creative Force taken into consideration and the entity becoming *one* with spiritual imports, it may use the powers and forces within to its own undoing.

"For the entity takes most every experience by intuition. Easily may the entity, by entering deep meditation raise the kundaline [the adjective of kundalini] forces in body to the third eye as to become a seeress; so that it may see the future and the past. But the law of such is that, unless these are used for constructive and never for selfish motives or purposes, they will bring more harm than good.

"There is the expression of creative energies that must be a part of the experience. Don't let the experiences of many turn thee aside, where and when it becomes necessary to raise such; and you will not be able to unless you live that you ask of and seek in others. Let that ye seek be that the law of the Lord God, which is manifested in the Christ, may be manifested through thee.

"If the body will do just that, it may become a credit to its own environ and all of those who have the pleasure and privilege of knowing the entity. Abusing it, ye will become a by-word, ye will become one not a credit to any.

"What will this entity do with these abilities? The choice may only be in self. Begin with the study of the Scripture as in Exodus 19:5, Deuteronomy 30, the whole of Romans, and John 14, 15, 16 and 17. Make these not only as things ye know but as things ye apply in principle and practice. Do that and come again - we would work with thee." (5028-1)

Physical Treatments that Aid Meditation

In reading 2072-2 Cayce indicated that life-force or kundalini meditation could be assisted and better coordinated if the practitioner would have spinal adjustments, he specifically identified the 3rd cervical plexus, the 9th thoracic plexus, and the 4th lumbar plexus. He also mentioned hydrotherapies, such as hot showers followed by a cold-water rinse along the spine. He encouraged epsom salt baths, and essential oil or tincture steam baths (or if no steam cabinet is available, a steamy bath with the shower curtain closed to seal in some of the steam with the essential oil or tincture. Cayce's most often recommended tinctures and oils were: Myrrh, Cedar Wood oil, Olive oil, Almond oil, Tolu Balsam, Eucalyptus oil, Tincture of Benzoin, Turpentine oil, and more. For more on this go to EdgarCayceProducts.com/Reference.html for the Edgar Cayce Remedy Reference Table.

He also supported the use of incense for those who naturally enjoyed such, accepting that not all meditators would fine incense helpful, some may even find it annoying.

In addition to hydrotherapies he often recommended an exercise for the cerebrospinal system. The exercise was nicknamed the "Head and Neck" exercise. Here's how that's done:

Tilt your head forward, chin toward your chest while feeling the stretch down your back and spine as your head goes forward. Do this slowly three times. Now, lift up your chin and tilt your head back three times, feeling the stretch down the front of your body and spine. Next, tilt the head to the right shoulder three times, feeling the stretch down the left side. Then, tilt your head to the left shoulder three times, feeling the stretch down the right side. Finally, slowly rotate your head three times clockwise and then three times counterclockwise. If you are standing, then your pelvis will counterbalance the weight of your head as your turn – it'll happen naturally. The key to this exercise is to feel the stretching all the way down your spine – from your neck to your tail bone. This loosens up the spinal column improving the flow of spinal fluid and nerve messages. If you have a neck or back condition, you must be careful to not aggravate the condition – in some conditions you may not be able to do this exercise, you know best.

Most anyone can learn to meditate and gradually
improve his/her skill with this important exercise for
the body and mind. In the beginning it helps if you
budget a time and place for your practice and stick to
it, for this helps the body and subconscious get into a
pattern, a habit of that time and that place being for
renew, rejuvenation, centering, and illuminating
oneself: physically, mentally, and spiritually.

"So long as life is active, there is the opportunity for
that soul to be moved by the
spirit of the God-consciousness."
–Edgar Cayce (3357-2)

Chapter 6
GOD-CONSCIOUSNESS

Spiritual breakthrough using passage in consciousness is about God-consciousness. The goal is to reach a level of consciousness that allows us to be *as aware of* God or the *Infinite, Collective Consciousness of the Universe* as we are of our own *finite, individual mind.* Imagine being as aware of God as we are of ourselves. This is the breakthrough we seek. But it is a difficult goal to realize. One of the greatest seekers of God-consciousness, the late Edgar Cayce taught: "Remember there is no shortcut to a consciousness of the God-force. It is part of your own consciousness, but it cannot be realized by the simple desire to do so. Too often there is the tendency to want it and expect it without applying spiritual truth through the medium of mental processes. This is the only way to reach the gate. There are no shortcuts in metaphysics. Life is learned within self. You don't profess it, you *learn* it."

Seekers of God-consciousness may include many more people than we imagine. Edgar Cayce considered people from many different backgrounds as true seekers of God-consciousness. He actually identifies certain biblical names and terms as codes for something much broader than we normally consider. As in the following quote: "This is the meaning, this should be the understanding to all: Those that *seek* are Israel. 'Think not to call thyselves the promise in Abraham. Know ye not that the Lord is able to raise up children of Abraham from the very stones?' So Abraham means *call*; so Israel means *those who seek*. How obtained the supplanter [Jacob] the name Israel? He wrestled with the angel, and he was face to face with seeking to know His way. So it is with us that are called and seek His face — We are Israel!"

In order to understand the nature of this breakthrough, we need to be familiar with our god-seeking heritage. Jews, Christians and Moslems all trace their heritage to Abraham and include the biblical stories in their religious literature. Let's review some great Bible stories and teachings, using Edgar Cayce's insights to help us gain a deeper understanding of the grand vista of God, man and woman, and God-consciousness.

Two Keys to Understanding Biblical Stories

In order to understand the mystical messages in the Bible, we need to keep two principles in mind as we read it.

First, the Bible is not only a historical record of a specific group of people, but is also *an allegory for each individual soul's journey*. It is a vision into the passages that *each* soul goes through in its quest for full enlightenment and eternal life. Therefore, when we read we should try to receive the stories as though they were personal insights and messages for ourselves, recalling our own past and foreshadowing our future. How can this be our past when we have only lived a short while? Because our *souls* have been alive from the beginning. As Jesus said, "Before Abraham was, I am." So too were we alive. In the Cayce discourses we find many supporting examples of this truth. Here are a few examples:

"The entity was in the beginning, when the Sons of God came together to announce to Matter a way being opened for the souls of men, the souls of God's creation...."

"In the beginning ... when the morning stars sang together, and the whispering winds brought the news of the coming of man's indwelling ... and man became the living soul — *the entity came into being with this multitude.*"

"For in the beginning, God said, 'Let there be light.' *You are one of those sparks of light*, with all the ability of Creation, with all the knowledge of God."

The Bible stories are *our* stories. We should read them as personal stories.

Second, the Bible contains not only the records of *physical* activities, it also contains metaphors of *inner-life* passages that occur as one awakens to "the Kingdom of God is within you." When a seemingly outer physical activity is described in a Bible story, let's consider what it might mean to our inner process of spiritual breakthrough — as though it were a dream, carrying a message behind the outer story. The physical becomes symbolic of something deeper and, as a dream or parable, it requires intuitive interpretation.

With these concepts in mind — namely, that the stories and teachings are *personal* and about *inner-life* processes — let's review some of the key stories in the Old and New Testaments. This background is important to our fuller understanding of the spiritual breakthrough process.

THE NATURE OF GOD

The Collective

Genesis begins, "In the beginning God ("Elohim") created the heavens and the earth. The Hebrew word

"Elohim" is a plural noun for "Deity." The use of the plural form reflects the collective, wholistic nature of God. When Elohim speak, "they" refer to themselves in the plural, such as: "Let *us* make him in *our* image, according to *our* likeness." Thus, Elohim is not a singular, supreme entity separate from the creation. God is the Collective, composed of the created ones while at the same time their source. We actually contribute to the composition of God. That is not to say that we compose all of God's being, but simply to say that a portion of God's being is us.

This truth is expressed in many of the Cayce readings. In one example, Cayce encourages one seeker to come to know that not only God is God but self is a portion of that Oneness.

As Jesus explained to Philip, "He who has seen me has seen the Father; how can you say, 'Show us the Father'? Do you not believe that I am in the Father and the Father in me? The words that I say to you I do not speak on my own authority; but the Father who dwells in me does His works. Believe me that I am in the Father and the Father in me; or else believe me for the sake of the works themselves." There was simply no way that Jesus could show the Father separate from himself. We and God are one. Again, we are not all of God's being, but we compose a portion of God and are ourselves composed of God. This is why the author of Genesis had to use the word "Elohim."

Some modern religious people do not like this concept and criticize it a chief characteristic of the New Age movement. The same criticism was leveled as Jesus during His time. The religious authorities could not accept that any man was so closely connected with God. It simply gave everyone their own direct line to God, requiring little of the authorities. But, as the Lord said in Jeremiah, He does not want anyone between Him and His created, no priest, no teachers. The Lord wants to teach each one of us directly.

"The Pharisees said, 'It is not for a good work that we stone you but for blasphemy; because you, being a man, make yourself God.' Jesus answered them, "Is it not written in your law, 'I said, you are gods'?" –John 10:33-34 Which Psalm 82 states: "God stands in the congregation of God; He judges among the gods. 'I said, Ye are gods, And all of you sons [and daughters] of the Most High.'" Psalm 82:1&6

Obviously, we are not fully conscious of this, and through this study we will discover why. Let's continue with the nature of God and the Beginning.

The Dark and the Light

In ancient teachings, God is composed of two aspects, a passive, impersonal quality and a dynamic, personal quality. The Genesis verse, "darkness was upon the face of the deep," refers to the first aspect of God. It is passive, quiet, impersonal, never changing and vast beyond imagining. "The deep" is a beautiful term to use for this aspect of God. Imagine was God's consciousness is like, and then select words to describe it. I don't think we could come up with a much better term than "the deep." The Genesis author also associates it with "darkness." But this is not in darkness in the sense of evil, rather in the sense of unknown, unseen, unmanifested.

This line is then followed by, "the Spirit of God moved upon the face of the waters" (no water had been created yet, so this may be interpreted as the waters of the deep, dark, infinite consciousness). The "Spirit of God," especially when it's moving, refers to a dynamic aspect of God. This is the Creator. It is personal, conscious, present and knowable. It communicates with man throughout the scriptures.

This dynamic aspect of God says, "Let there be light," a metaphor for consciousness. It is the Logos. And the light, or consciousness, was good, and was separated from the darkness, or unconsciousness. The darkness is subsequently called "Night," symbolizing the deep stillness of the unconscious. The light is called "Day," symbolizing the seen and the active. Following this pattern, an ancient Hebrew day began at sundown, recalling that darkness was before light, unconsciousness before consciousness, night before day, sleep before wakefulness.

When we are too much in the life of the Day, we are out of balance. Unconsciousness and the stillness of the Night are equally important to our health and well-being. Sleep, rest, the inward nature of prayer and meditation, and our stillness while listening are as important to us as wakefulness, activity and speaking. This is expressed by the Psalmist as, "Day unto day pours forth speech, and night unto night reveals knowledge." Our going in to our inner consciousness and our coming out to our outer consciousness is the balance of the inner places and unseen forces with the outer places and seen forces. We, as portions of God, are composed of both, and need to have these in balance.

Spirit

It's important that we understand "spirit" since it is key to our breakthrough. "Ruwach" is the Hebrew word used here. It literally means "wind," as in "the spirit [wind] of God moved upon the face of the waters." Wind is a poetic expression for the unseen force *behind* a manifested condition. We see the leaves and branches of a tree move and we know the unseen wind is the cause. As Jesus says to Nicodemus, "the wind blows where it will, and you hear the sound of it but do not know from where it comes or to where it goes; so is everyone who is born of the spirit."

In Jesus' discussion with the woman at the well, he says "God is Spirit, and those who worship Him must worship in spirit...." The one, great Spirit is composed of our spirits, and true worship, or attunement, is achieved by "moving" into the spirit, as opposed to being predominantly conscious in the body and the mind. The disciple John begins his recording of the Revelation with, "I was in the spirit on the Lord's day...." The Cayce discourses also speak to this important principle, "For the image in which man was created is spiritual, as He thy Maker is spiritual." (1257-1)

Throughout the Old Testament, the *Spirit* of God brings two great gifts: *life* and *wisdom*. In Job, Elihu acknowledges that the Spirit has given life to us when he says, "the Spirit of God hath made me." God's Spirit gives life to all, including minerals, plants and animals. Where there is Spirit, there is life.

The Spirit's wisdom-giving power is expressed again by Elihu when he says to Job, "It is the spirit in a man, the breath of the Almighty, that makes him understand." We also see how the spirit is known to bring wisdom when Pharaoh, after being astonished by Joseph's wisdom, asks his counselors, "Can we find such a man as this, in whom is the spirit of God? Since God has shown you all this, there is none so discreet and wise as you are." And in Jesus' hours before the crucifixion, he teaches that when he departs from the earth, the Holy Spirit will come and "teach you all things, and bring all things to your remembrance." Where there is spirit, there is wisdom.

God, therefore, is collective, containing all and within all. It is unconscious and conscious. It is spirit and, as such, gives life and wisdom.

By the way, when I use the neutral pronoun "It" for God, it is because I simply cannot convey the correct impression of God by using either of the other two pronouns in our language, "he" or "she." God contains both the feminine and masculine. God is both Mother and Father. Further, God is not nearly so personal as the he/she pronouns imply. God is not *a person*, as we would think of a person. Therefore, "It" is, to my mind, the best pronoun. Of course, if I were true to the author of Genesis, I'd use "They," in keeping with the plural noun *Elohim*. And though I truly believe "They" is an excellent pronoun for God, it does at times become awkward and tends to cause us to think of God as many, when God is one. "Hear, Oh Israel, the Lord thy God, the Lord is one." Therefore, "It" will have to do.

OUR NATURE

Spirit and Soul

There is a subtle but significant distinction between *spirit* and *soul*. Spirit, as we have just reviewed, is associated with the wind, while soul corresponds to the breath. The spirit, like the wind, is *universal* and free; whereas the soul, like the breath, is more *individual* and contained. They are similar, both being air. As the wind moves by one's nostrils, it can be inhaled and become personal breath. In the first chapter of Genesis, we read that God created *adam* in Its image (spirit). In chapter two, the "Lord God" (Yahweh Elohim) creates adam again by breathing the *breath* of life into him/her, and he becomes "a living being [soul]." Notice how the "spirit [wind] of God" first created us in Its image, and later, we became living souls by the "breath" of the Lord God. Spirit is the wind; soul is the breath. One is more universal, the other is more individual. In the Cayce readings, the spirit is the life force, while the soul is that unique portion of each entity that is the sum total of all the entity has done with its gift of life. Soul is our unique story, our individualness.

Additionally, spirit is considered unchanging, whereas soul is developmental. The soul grows, learns, and becomes the companion to God. The spirit is the same yesterday, today and tomorrow. It is life – eternal, unchanging life. Spirit is also considered the source of wisdom. When St. John says he is "in the spirit," he is referring to a process whereby he awakens to and attunes to the more spiritual aspect of his being; then, in turn, attunes that to the essence of all life, the Collective Spirit (Elohim). Understanding this is helps us break through to the spiritual.

Flesh

As we enter the earth realm, another quality is added to our composition – flesh. This adds blood to the metaphor of wind and breath. Now blood must permeate the lungs to get life from the breath, soul, which, in turn, gets its life from the wind, *spirit*.

Flesh (or our identification with it) is that portion of our being that separates us most from God. At one point during the great fall in Genesis, God says, "My spirit will not always be with man, for he is flesh." God is not flesh. God is spirit. In order to fully know God, one must break through to the spirit. And, when "the great and terrible day of the Lord" comes, it is terrible precisely because unspiritualized flesh will have little part in it. Those who have not regained some sense of their spiritual selves will be in anguish over their fleshness. Jesus described it to his disciples as, "weeping and gnashing of teeth."

Let's review the story of creation, our beginnings.

OUR GENESIS

In the beginning God creates us in Its own image, "Let *us* make man [adam] in *our* image, after *our* likeness…. So God created man [adam] in His own image, in the image of God He created him; male and female He created them." In this verse the Hebrew word for man is "adam." This word is often translated as "reddish" or "ruddy," but it also means "persons" or "people" collectively, and can mean an "indefinite someone." It is important to note in this verse that adam is male and female in one, androgynous. It is not until later when the "Lord God" creates adam "out of the dust of the earth," in other words, *in the flesh*, that these parts are separated. When this occurs, the name "adam" takes on the meaning we most commonly associate with this word, "ruddy" or "red," resulting from the blood in flesh.

It is important to realize that adam was first made in the image of God, which we know is not flesh, but spirit, female and male in oneness, unconscious and conscious united. Then, symbolized by the changing of the name of the creator from "God" to "Lord God" and, subsequently, to simply "Lord," we see the descent from direct God-consciousness to self-consciousness. This is the descent from pure spirit to spiritualized flesh to disconnected flesh, at which time death takes hold. Understanding this helps us breakthrough to the original consciousness and condition.

Another important point about this creation is that it is a *group* creation, not just the creation of one famous person. "Adam" at this stage of the creation is referring to an original group of souls created by God in God's image, and subsequently made in spiritualized flesh by the Lord God, then into mortal flesh by the Lord. According to the Cayce readings, the souls, those godlings within the One God, entered the earth in five places, five nations, five races; in one, they were called "Adam," and this is the story of those souls.

At this point in Genesis, God has created everything in thought, in the mind of God, but not physically — all existed in God's consciousness. This is symbolized in the passage that comes *after* the seven days of creation: "Now no shrub of the field was yet in the earth [physically], and no plant of the field had yet sprouted, for the Lord God [note the name change] had not sent rain upon the earth; and there was no man [in flesh] to cultivate the ground." Yet, we know the heaven, earth and Adam had been created. The author is trying to convey to us that they had been created only in the mind of God not in form.

The original creation occurred *in God's infinite consciousness*. This was our natural home before entering the flesh. It is what is spoken of in Jesus' prayer to God, "And now, glorify Thou me together with Thyself, Father, with the glory which I had with Thee *before the world was*." And it is that realm spoken of when Jesus says to us, "I go to prepare a place for you ... that where I am there you may be also. And you know the way where I am going." Now, like many of us who are so much into physical consciousness, the disciple Thomas challenges this statement, "Lord, we do not know where you are going. How do we know the way?" But we do know the way. Deep within us is our true nature. Deep within us we remember the original home, and we know the way. Each of us was there in the beginning. Each of us was originally created in the image and likeness of God. Within us that original nature lives and intuitively knows its way home. As Jesus said, "No one ascend to heaven but he who has already descended from it, even the Son of Man."

Yin and Yang (female and male)

As we touched on earlier, ancient teachings hold that the One is composed of two aspects: that of the *dark* — meaning unseen, deep, and from out of which comes the other aspect, *light* — meaning seen, present and active. In the Eastern philosophies the terms "yin" and "yang" are used to express these characteristics. Yin is a feminine principle, yang a masculine one.

If we simply look objectively at the physical bodies of a female and male (the ultimate manifestation of these two aspects), we see the reflection of their innate qualities. A female's sexual organs are deep *within* her torso, a male's outside his. A female body has more *inner* processes than a male, such as menstrual cycles, conception, gestation, and milk production. The female reflects the characteristics of the inner aspect of God. Thus she is a reflection of the dark, unknown, unseen, unmanifested God, the yin. She represents the unconscious, sleep, and "Night" in Genesis, thus, "the Moon and the Stars." This would also imply that the feminine is the wind, the spirit, especially since she is the conceiver, the "life-giver." On the other side, the male reflects the characteristics of the outer, manifested God. Thus, he is a reflection of the active, changing, personal, present God. He represents the conscious, wakefulness; "Day" in Genesis, thus the Sun. He is the "tiller of the soil," the doer, the conqueror. This would also imply that he is then the reflection of the breath, the soul, especially since he is the changing, developing "doer." Our original nature was composed of both these aspects in one being, but soon these were to be separated.

The Separation of the Genders

Our fall from the original place of being is allegorically presented as the separation of the sexes and the eating of the "Fruit of the Tree of the Knowledge of Good and Evil," which symbolizes consuming knowledge without understanding. The Cayce readings state it this way, "...seek not for knowledge alone. For, look – LOOK – what it brought Eve. Look rather for that wisdom which was eventually founded in she [Mary] that was addressed as 'the handmaid of the Lord'...." (2072-10)

Because of our continued pull toward self-consciousness, we lose God-consciousness and *descend* into the narrow realm of the physical world. In Genesis 2:7, not God, but the "Lord God" creates us again, *after* the seven days of creation. This time we are created in spiritualized, physical form. "Then the Lord God formed man [adam, still male and female in one] of dust from the ground, and breathed into his nostrils the breath of life; and man became a living being [physically]." –Genesis 2:7

The author of Genesis tells us that now that man became flesh, he/she was so separated from the spiritual realm and God, that he/she was lonely. As the Lord God observes, "It is not good that the man [adam] should be alone; I shall make him a helper fit for him." Lord God brought all the creatures of the earth before Adam, but there was none found companionable with this god-man in flesh. We were truly out of our natural element; as Jesus said, we are "not of this world." But, having made the descent from heaven, we now had to find a better way to live in the physical realm.

Therefore, the Lord God caused a deep sleep to fall upon the androgynous man, and while he slept took one of his ribs and closed up its place with flesh; and the rib which the Lord God had taken from the man he made into a woman and brought her to the man. Then the man said, "This at last is bone of my bones and flesh of my flesh; she shall be called Woman, because she was taken out of Man."

In this deep sleep, the Lord God went into the inner places of the god-man and separated the two parts, bringing out one side of the whole being. These two sides could now be true help-meets one to the other. In Adam's poetic verse, the word "Man" is no longer "adam" but "ish," meaning male. The word "Woman" is "ishshah" (also, *ishah*) meaning female. They that were one in "adam" are now separated into "ish" and "ishshah," man and woman. The male retained the name "Adam" and the female was called "Chavvah," meaning "life-giver," eventually, "Eve," meaning "life, living, lively."

As the great depth psychologist Carl Jung noted, we are only expressions of part of ourselves. If we project the masculine, then the feminine is in the unconscious. If we project the feminine, then the masculine is in the unconscious. To be whole, we must all get in touch with our other portion.

Separation from God

In the beginning, adam represented the spirit-soul entity. This entity was, and remains, that portion of our being that is the companion to God. It is both male and female, and is in the image of God. We were composed of spirit (God), individualness (soul), and free-will (the gift of God). However, as we children of God used free-will to experience the infinite realms of the Cosmos, we became increasingly self-conscious, losing much of our God-consciousness. Eventually, some of us, not all, descended into the earth, the 3-dimensional world, and entered flesh. This required that we be made again in the flesh. Thus, we were formed out of the dust of the earth and our twin aspects were divided into yin and yang, male and female. We were naked, but at first our nakedness was not known to us and the Lord God did not call it our attention.

The Origin of Sin/Evil

The Lord God had commanded adam not to eat from the Tree of the Knowledge of Good and Evil, saying "for in the day you eat from it, you shall surely die." Up to this point, we were immortal beings, in the image of the immortal God. However, the further we moved from consciousness of our connectedness with the Eternal One, the more we lost connectedness to the source of Life. Adam and Eve began to live too completely in the flesh, losing touch with the life-giving Spirit. They began to reverse the flow of the Life Force, the élan vital, bringing it further into self-consciousness. This became so acute that, according to the Cayce readings, we actually experienced a death of the spirit. To put it another way, we died to the spiritual influence.

Another significant piece to this puzzling death was the growth of something *other than God*.

Self and the Serpent

The serpent in the Garden represents SELF. It is self without regard for the Whole or for other beings. It is the self that seeks self-gratification, self-glorification, self-aggrandizement, self-centeredness. But in order for the potential companions of God to be true companions, they had to have a strong sense of self. As the Cayce readings state it: "That he may know himself to be himself and yet one with the Father [the Creator]." Therefore, despite the dangers inherent in the development of self-consciousness, it was allowed because it was and remains the way to full realization of our role as divine companions. Yet, it often becomes a stumbling block.

The serpent, "more subtle than any other creature the Lord God had made," symbolizes two aspects of our being: 1) the life force, called the *kundalini* in ancient Sanskrit texts; and, 2) the selfish self (especially when not cooperating with the Whole).

In the Garden, our selfishness (the serpent) convinces the two other aspects of our consciousness (Adam and Eve) that they could safely ignore God's guidance, and would *not* die, as God had stated. Ignoring God resulted in a narrowing of consciousness and the life force – symbolized by the serpent coming down out of the tree and crawling on the ground.

Adam, Eve and the serpent (all aspects of ourselves) fall from grace and lose the comfort of the garden. The Tree of Life, symbolizing immortality, is now protected from us, so we can't become eternal *terrestrial* beings when we are meant to be eternal *celestial* beings. And we now enter the cycle of birth, life, death, and rebirth.

This is further symbolized in Eve's conception of two beings: Cain and Abel. Cain literally means the "acquired" one (our forming egos). Abel means "a breath," or soul (our spiritually aware self). Of course, God favors the offerings of our souls more than our egos, as symbolized in Abel's offering as opposed to Cain's. However, Cain (ego) is angered by this and kills Abel (soul). Yet, when the Lord comes to Cain, He says, "Why are you angry, and why has your countenance fallen? If you do well, will you not be accepted? And if you do not do well, sin is couching at the door [of your consciousness]; its desire is for you, but *you must master it.*" –Genesis 4:6-7 RSV

This is the great call to us. Yes, self-consciousness is dangerous. It may lead to self-centeredness and loss of union with the Whole. But it is such a wonderful gift that it is worth the trials. We simply must, as the Lord God said in the Garden, "Subdue the earth [i.e., our self-centered urges]." And, as the Lord said to our Cain-self, "You must master it (selfishness)." By gaining control of this gift, we will come to know ourselves to be ourselves and yet one with the Whole.

STAGES TO REGAINING
GOD-CONSCIOUSNESS

"Thus as you take hold of the thought of God Consciousness, it may be just as pregnant a concept in mind as a baby in our body."

In order to identify the stages of resurrection or rebirth in the spirit, let's enumerate the stages of our fall, and see how they can be turned around to bring resurrection. There are three major changes that brought on our loss of God-consciousness and all three can be turned around to regain it.

1) The death of the influence of the Elohim Spirit and the rise of self.

2) The reverse of the flow of the Life Force.

3) The witness against us.

Let's examine these in detail.

1. We died to the spirit and gave birth to the self. The spirit and the universal consciousness of God is the true source and nature of Life, so when we died to it, we lost immortality and wisdom. And, since God is spirit, we also lost consciousness of God. This is symbolized by the name changes for God and by our being denied access to the Tree of Life. We became mortal. We also began to develop an even stronger sense of self, to the point that we lost awareness of self's connectedness to the Whole – God and other souls. This mounting sense of self separated us from direct contact with God, and is symbolized by our emergence into a single physical body, with singular gender. What was collective and united is now singular and separated. In order to regain God-consciousness, this movement from the spirit to the self must be turned around.

Jesus says to Nicodemus, "Unless one is born anew, he cannot see the kingdom of God. ... That which is born of the flesh is flesh, and that which is born of the Spirit is spirit." In this teaching we are given a great insight. We have been born of flesh and, using the old terms, that makes us "sons and daughters of man." However, we must also be born of the Spirit, making us "sons and daughters of God." During our physical lives, we should strive to experience the second birth, the birth of the spirit. This is spoken of and symbolized many times in both Testaments, beginning in the Garden itself. (Remember now, we are to consider physical activities as metaphors of what happens *within* consciousness. All the characters in these stories are also elements of our own soul development.)

At the time of the loss of the Garden, God prophesies that Eve, and all women after her, will give birth only through much effort and pain, but that her line will one day give birth to the savior, to the one who will subdue (or reverse) the serpent's influence. In our personal experience, that translates to this: our feminine, inner, deeper self — with all its unseen forces and spiritual powers — will conceive, gestate and deliver a new consciousness which will raise the serpent up, be "born anew," and regain what was lost. This will be our spiritual selves.

The story of Mary's conception and delivery of a new child is perhaps the fullest expression of this idea. Let's review the angel Gabriel's description of what will happen to her:

"Behold, you will conceive in your womb [the womb of our inner consciousness], and bear a child.... He will be great, and will be called the Son of the Most High; and the Lord God will give him the throne ... and he will reign over the house of Jacob forever; and his kingdom will have no end." And Mary said to the angel, "How can this be, since I am a virgin?" [From the earthly perspective, as a daughter of man, how can this be done? Almost the same reaction Nicodemus had to Jesus' teaching about spiritual birth.] And the angel answered and said to her, "The Holy Spirit will come upon you, and the power of the Most High will overshadow you; and for that reason the holy offspring shall be called the son of God." –Luke 1:35 RSV

The description of this conception is reminiscent of deep, meditative, mystical experience — "The Holy Spirit will come upon you, and the power of the Most High will overshadow you." It also calls to mind other wonderful expressions of this experience:

"And it shall come to pass that I will *pour out my spirit upon all flesh*; and your sons and daughters shall prophesy, your old shall dream dreams, and your young shall see visions." –Joel 2:28 & Acts 2:17 RSV

"...suddenly a sound came from heaven like the rush of a mighty wind [spirit], and it filled all the house where they were sitting. And there appeared to them tongues as of fire, distributed and resting on each one of them. And they were all *filled with the Holy Spirit*...." – Acts 2:2 RSV

"How precious is thy steadfast love, O God! The children of men take refuge in the shadow of thy wings. They feast on the abundance of thy inner place, and thou givest them drink from the river of thy delights. For within thee is the fountain of life; in thy light do we see light." – Psalm 36:8 RSV

Another important expression of this idea comes as Jesus nears the end of his physical ministry. At the last Passover dinner, Jesus says that his soul has become troubled. Later, as he sought to calm the troubled spirits of his disciples — they were beginning to realize he would soon be leaving them — he compared their feelings to those of a woman in labor: She has sorrow because her hour of pain and struggle are upon her, but when she is delivered of the child, she no longer remembers the anguish, for the joy that a child is born.

So it is with us in our hour of delivery of our spiritual child. Each of us has conceived this spiritual being within our hearts and minds. We have nourished it in the wombs of our consciousnesses. Now it is time for us to deliver it, and the pain and struggle of this is upon us. However, once delivered of it, we will rejoice that a child is born — not a child of man, but a child of God. Our spirit will be *present*, and will be able to attune to God directly, which is the purpose of spiritual breakthrough.

In the Revelation we also see a woman in labor, a heavenly woman:

"And a great portent appeared in heaven, a woman clothed with the Sun, with the Moon under her feet, and on her head a crown of twelve stars; she was with child and she cried out in her pangs of birth, in anguish for delivery." –Revelation 12:1 RSV

She, as well as Mary, symbolizes the fulfillment of God's promise to Eve. Out of her will come the savior, who will overcome selfishness and reunite us with the Whole. Like Mary, she also represents for us the process of spiritual breakthrough:

We have already *conceived* our redeemer, our messiah, our *spiritual* being within our hearts and minds — or we wouldn't even be studying these things. Now we must fully realize it by giving birth to it, letting it become fully alive and present. This requires that we lay down our outer selves and give birth to our inner selves. We must subjugate the flesh, the earthly portion of our being, to the Higher Forces, and give place or space in our consciousness and life for our reborn spiritual being. As Jesus expresses it, "Unless a grain of wheat falls into the earth and dies, it remains alone; but if it dies, it bears much fruit. He who loves his life loses it, and he who hates his life in this world will keep it for eternal life."

We must yield to the will of the spirit within us, allowing it to have expression in our lives. If we will seek its way more than our own, eventually it will be fully manifest. We will be, once again, spiritual beings, even while in the physical world. As Jesus states it, "When you have lifted up the son of man, then you will know...." When we have raised our earthly selves to the level of consciousness of our heavenly selves, then we will know what it's all about and who we really are.

2. We reversed the flow of the Life Force. Our kundalini energy was used to physically manifest and breed. It flows down our spines and out to the world, mostly in gratification and self-exaltation. This is, literally, the fall of the serpent.

Moses (symbolizing one "drawn out" of the unconscious) leads the seekers out of material captivity (symbolized by Egypt) and away from the control of Pharaoh (symbolic of the ego self), across the wilderness to the Mount of God, where we reconnect with God and eventually enter the Promised Land. One of the great signs that Moses performs, following God's guidance, is to raise the serpent, and all who look upon it are healed from its bite. While teaching Nicodemus about "heavenly things," Jesus refers to this great sign saying, "No one has ascended into heaven but he who descended from heaven, even the Son of man. And as Moses lifted up the serpent in the wilderness, even so must the Son of man be lifted up, that whoever believes may in him have eternal life." If we interpret this teaching for us as individuals, it shows that through misuse of the life-force (kundalini, serpent power) and self-consciousness (the serpent, dragon, Satan, etc.), we descended from heaven and lost consciousness of our nature as sons and daughters of God, believing ourselves to be no more than sons and daughters of other humans. If we wish to ascend to heaven and regain our heritage as children of God, then we must raise the life-force (raise the serpent) and raise the consciousness of our physical selves (raise the son of man) so that we may once again have the glory that was ours before the world was, and live eternally with God.

3. We are a witness against ourselves. Our conscience knows what we have done. The resulting guilt, self-condemnation, and self-doubt holds us from fully entering into God's all-knowing presence. This is expressed in the story of Job. Let's take a moment to review key parts of this story.

The story of Job begins, "Now there was a day when the sons [and daughters] of God came to present themselves before the Lord, and Satan also came among them." As a result of our movement into selfness and the flesh, we are not able to come into the presence of God, even though we are "the sons [and daughters] of God." We therefore present ourselves to "the Lord" (the Hebrew is "Yahweh"). Even then, because of our changes, when we come before the Lord, we bring Satan with us. Satan here symbolizes our growing self-centered nature, in opposition to God and the Collective. Literally, the name Satan means "the accuser." The Lord asks Satan, our selfness, "Have you considered my servant Job, that there is none like him on the earth, a blameless and upright man, who fears God and turns away from evil?" Our selfness then witnesses against the goodness symbolized in Job, saying that if the Lord puts forth His hand and touches anything of Job's possessions or Job's flesh, he will curse the Lord to His face. Is Job righteous because his physical life is comfortable, or is he righteous because he loves God, loves the spirit, more than the temporary pleasures of the physical, self-centered life? The Lord tells Satan to test him. Satan tries Job terribly, but Job does not curse the Lord for his physical pain and loss. Job's friends also accuse him of sin, since otherwise these bad things would not have come upon him and his family. But Job searches his heart and finds no evil in himself. Then, Job cries to the Lord and the Lord comes to him. They engage in a dynamic conversation, coming to know one another directly. All that Job lost is restored a hundredfold. But, better than that, Job has come to know the Lord directly, and the Lord has come to know Job.

Satan, our self-centered selves, is a witness against us. When we come before the Lord, the all-knowing consciousness, we bring this accuser with us.

Another example of this is found in the Old Testament Book of Zechariah, when Joshua is presented to the Lord. "... Joshua the high priest standing before the angel of the Lord, and Satan standing at his right hand to *accuse* him. And the Lord said to Satan, 'The Lord rebuke you, O Satan! The Lord who has chosen Jerusalem rebuke you! Is not this a brand plucked from the fire?' Now Joshua was standing before the angel, clothed with filthy garments, and the angel said to those who were standing before him, 'Remove the filthy garments from him.' And to him he said, 'Behold, *I have taken your iniquity away* from you, and I will clothe you with festal robes.'" Later, the Lord says, "I will remove the guilt of this land in a single day." And a little later, the Lord says this is accomplished "not by might, nor by power, but by my Spirit." The garments of our consciousness are soiled from our self-centered activities and thoughts, but the spirit can and will cleanse them in a moment, and rebuke the accuser in our minds.

Perhaps the clearest example of the need to rid our consciousness of the accuser is found in the Revelation. The Revelation is more than a book of prophecy; it is an insight into the very nature of our *inner* passage into full God-consciousness. As the Cayce readings put it: "The Revelation ... is a description of ... thy own consciousness...." "Why, then, is it presented, ye ask, in the form of symbols? These are for those that were, or will be, or may become, through the seeking, those initiated into an understanding of the glories that may be theirs if they will but put into work, into activity, that they know in the present. ... These [the symbols] represent self; self's body-physical, self's body-mental, self's body-spiritual...."

Earlier in this study, a scene from the Revelation was described in which the divine pregnant woman is striving to be delivered of her heavenly baby. Swirling about her is a red dragon. This dragon is the full grown serpent of the Garden, Satan, the accuser. It is the self-seeking aspect of our being. It is ready to devour our new consciousness in a belly of self-doubt and self-condemnation. But the archangel Michael, the Lord and Protector of the Way (also an aspect of our being), fights with this dragon and drives it out of heaven, out of our higher consciousness. Then, a loud voice from heaven (our higher consciousness) cries out,

"Now the salvation and the power and the kingdom of our God and the authority of his Anointed One have come, for the accuser of our brethren has been thrown down, who accuses them day and night before our God. And they have conquered him by the blood of the Lamb and by the word of their testimony, for they loved not their lives even unto death. Rejoice then, O heaven and you that dwell therein! But woe to you, O earth and sea, for the devil has come down to you in great wrath, because he knows that his time is short!" –Revelation 12:10-12

We must drive out of our minds this accuser, this self-doubt, this self-condemning influence, if we are to fully regain God-consciousness. Our consciousness will rejoice when it is done, for now our divine feminine can safely deliver our spiritual nature.

Jesus and God-Consciousness

The life of Jesus connects deeply with these stages in the regaining of God-consciousness, and it wouldn't be going too far to say that he *initiated* them.

Perhaps the main contribution of his life was to serve as the *pattern* for being connected with God-consciousness. Having lost that connection ourselves, we were very weak in the area of spirit, but growing strong in the areas of the physical and the mental. We needed help regaining the spiritual influences and consciousness. Cayce puts it this way:

"One finds self a body, a mind, a soul; each with its own attributes and its activity in the earth. An entity, then, is a pattern of that which is also a spiritual fact; Father, Son, Holy Spirit. These are one, just as an individual entity is one. An entity, then, is the pattern of divinity in materiality, or in the earth. As man found himself out of touch with that complete consciousness of the oneness of God, it became necessary that the will of God, the Father, be made manifested, that a pattern be introduced into man's consciousness. Thus the son of man came into the earth..." (3357-1)

Jesus taught us much about the *way of spirit* in responding to others and to situations that arise. In relation to casting out the witness against us, he showed us that to be free of that influence, we need only *cease doing any accusing ourselves*. Coming into a society that held only negative feelings towards lepers, prostitutes, foreign soldiers, and tax-collectors, he accepted and loved them all. He showed us that *the way of spirit* lies not in trying to eliminate in ourselves (and others!) whatever the accuser might point to. Instead, he taught us to *love* one another and ourselves and to subdue the accuser's voice of condemning judgment.

Even at the end of his life, Jesus was teaching us about strengthening our connection with spirit. The crucifixion is symbolic of much more than restitution for sin. In its deepest meaning it is the way to resurrection. Let's take a closer look at the significant activities and discussions leading up to and following the crucifixion.

It begins at the Last Supper. That Passover night and meal has its origins in ancient Egypt on the night the Angel of Death came upon all incarnate beings in

Egypt, exempting only those who had the blood of the lamb upon the doorpost of their house (symbolic of the doorpost of their consciousness). This freed the seekers from bondage to the ruler of Earth, allowing them to go to the Mount of God and the Promised Land.

So, now, Jesus and his disciples relive this moment, breaking bread and sharing wine together — *symbols* of breaking flesh and shedding blood. As the evening unfolds, Jesus becomes troubled. He says, "And now my soul is troubled because my hour has come upon me. And what should I do? Call to my Father in heaven and ask Him to deliver me from this hour? No, for this hour have I come." Yet, a few hours later in the garden he is troubled again, "My soul is very sorrowful, even to death... Abba (literally, "Papa"), Father, all things are possible to Thee; remove this cup from me; yet not what I will, but what Thou wilt." This is the outer man wrestling with the great transition from self-determined, physical man to God-centered, spiritual man. The physical, outer, earthy self does not inherit the kingdom of heaven. The spiritual, inner, heavenly self inherits the kingdom. Thus, the deep meaning behind the ancient Hebrew concept of the blood-sacrifice relates directly to the subjugation of flesh to the spirit. Breaking through the flesh encasement (shedding the blood) yields the spirit and gives it its rightful place as the dominant, true self. As the process is completed, the physical self cries, "Why hast thou forsaken me?" But the intuitive soul says, "Into thy hands I commend my spirit," and gives up the flesh life for the spirit life. Now we enter into the tomb, the cave, the coffin – death, sleep and the dark unconscious. Then, by the unseen powers of the Spirit, we rise again, reborn. Only now we are predominantly spiritual beings manifesting physically, rather than physical beings with spiritual attributes.

As Job was restored a hundredfold, as Jesus came again to eat fish and honey with his disciples on the beach after his resurrection, and all that was lost in the Genesis Garden was regained in the "new heaven and new earth" of the Revelation. So will we be restored. The Tree of Life, the Water of Life, and the new dwelling will be given to us to "take freely."

In the ancient Egyptian temple of the Great Pyramid, the coffin in the upper chamber is empty. When the women came to anoint Jesus' body, they found that the tomb held no decaying body. All initiates of the ancient mystery schools were taught *there is no death*. That is, there is no death when the spirit is present and predominant.

When we lay aside our personal, earthly, physical interests — even though we feel "forsaken" — and commend ourselves into God's hands (the Spirit's life-giving and wisdom-giving power), we rise up again, a new person, one with God, God-conscious again — fully integrating body, mind, soul and spirit and attuning them to the Great Spirit, the Elohim, God. Now what was separated is rejoined. What was lost is found. What was dead, lives.

"Dost thou seek to enter into the glories of the Father? Whosoever will may come, may take of the water of life freely – even as flows from the throne of the Lamb. ...If ye will accept, the blood cleanses from all unrighteousness. Saves self from what? To what are ye called? To know that only from the falling away of self may ye be saved – unto the glorifying of self in Him may ye be saved. Then, whosoever will, come!" (EC 281-16)

Gustave Dore's Revelation Image

"As [one] sets itself to accomplish
that which is of a creative influence …
no longer is the entity under the law of cause and
effect or karma, but rather in grace."
- Edgar Cayce (2800-2)

Chapter 7
FRUITS OF THE SPIRIT

In his reading numbered 5752-3, Edgar Cayce reveals the surprising consciousness and vibration that results from practicing the fruits of the Spirit. It's like this: when we assimilate these fruits into our thoughts, words, and actions we become the Spirit. Here's his reading on this:

"Do that which is good, for there has been given in the consciousness of all the fruits of the spirit: fellowship, kindness, gentleness, patience, long-suffering, love; these be the fruits of the spirit. Against such there is no law. Doubt, fear, avarice, greed, selfishness, self-will; these are the fruits of the evil forces. Against such there IS a law. Self-preservation, then, should be in the fruits of the spirit, as ye seek through any channel to know more of the path from life to life, from good to good, from death unto life, from evil unto good. Seek and ye shall find. Meditate on the fruits of the Spirit in the inner secrets of the consciousness, and the cells in the body become aware of the awakening of the life in their activity

157

through the body. In the mind, the cells of the mind become aware of the life in the spirit. The spirit of life maketh not afraid. Then, know the way; for those that seek may find."

According to the disciple Paul, as he wrote in Galatians 5:22-23, the fruits of the Spirit are love, joy, peace, long-suffering, gentleness, goodness, faith, meekness, and temperance.

Cayce adds: patience, mercy, kindness, and forgiveness. In his reading 1336-1 he explains that, "only in the fruits of the spirit may the *true meaning* of life's experience and the purposes of life ... be understood ... as a practical application ... in thy daily life with thy daily experience with thy fellow man."

THE FRUITS OF THE SPIRIT
Love, Peace, & Joy
Kindness, Gentleness, & Mercy
Faith , Meekness, & Humility
Goodness & Temperance
Patience, Forgiveness, & Long-suffering

A major Catholic Bible translates Paul's passage quit differently from all Protestant translations, including the addition of three new fruits! This translation into English was a literal, word-for-word translation of the ancient Latin Vulgate Bible, translated by Jerome from the years 382 to 405! The Latin Vulgate was translated from Hebrew and Chaldean Scriptures, which comprise the Christian

Old Testament, and the Greek records of the Gospels, Epistles, and Revelation, which comprise the Christian New Testament.

This Catholic translation from Latin to English was published prior to the 1611 publication of the King James Version, upon which most modern Protestant Bibles are based. The Catholic English New Testament was first published in 1582 by the British College at Rheims. Later, in 1609, the British College at Douay, published the Catholic Old Testament. Thus, this Bible is called the Douay-Rheims Version (DRV). Here is that most unusual translation.

"But the fruit of the Spirit is charity, joy, peace, patience, benignity, goodness, longanimity, mildness, faith, modesty, continency, and chastity." (DRV)

As you can see, "love" is "charity," and not surprisingly the King James Bible uses "charity," but it's the only modern bible translation to do so.

Now most of us squirm at the thought of "longsuffering," and that term is not in this old translation, rather the word is "longanimity." Webster's dictionary defines "longanimity" as *forbearance*, as in patient endurance. Which is much more comfortable a practice than longsuffering.

We also find "continency" in this old list. We may think of continency in this context as *self-control* over human urges, cravings, compulsions, desires, and passions—of which humans have many. Some especially apply this term to indulgence of the sexual appetite. In the Cayce readings sex with love is ideal but sex without love is slipping toward self-gratification, and one must be mindful of their motivations and purposes. Of course there are other appetites beyond sex that can consume a person and damage their body, life, and relationships. Continency calls for honest, mindful *self-control* in these matters. It is possible that continency correlates to the modern term *temperance*. But temperance is most commonly associated with excesses in eating and drinking.

Some correlate continency with *chastity*—but that would mean *abstinence*, not mindful, self-controlled moderation and appropriateness.

"Mildness" in the old list could easily correlate to *meekness* in the current list.

The word "benignity" reveals just how literal the translation was from the Latin; this word having the Latin root for "well-born," which was believed to naturally produce a manner and tone that was kind and gentle. It has a clear connotation of civility because it is applied in interact *with* others in social settings and conversations.

Adjusting our habits, our patterns of thought, speech, and action in daily application of the fruits of the Spirit gradually creates a new vibration and consciousness within us. We are what we think, say, and do.

Spirit

Some consideration should be given to understanding what Spirit is. The first use of the term in connection with the Lord is found in Numbers 11:24-25. In this passage, the Lord's Spirit came upon Moses in the form of a descending cloud. Moses had gathered seventy good men with him. The Lord took some of the Spirit that was upon Moses, and put it on the seventy men. As a result, these men began to prophesy, but only while the Spirit was upon them. Here's the passage:

"And Moses went out and gave the people the words of the Lord; and he took seventy of the responsible men of the people, placing them round the Tent. Then the Lord came down in the cloud and had talk with him, and put on the seventy men some of the spirit that was on him; now when the spirit came to rest on them, they were like prophets, but only at that time." (Numbers 11:24-25, Bible in Basic English, BBE)

The full term "Spirit of the Lord" does not appear in the Bible until Judges 3:10. In this verse, the people of Israel were in captivity and were crying to the Lord to deliver them.

"When the people of Israel cried to the Lord, the Lord raised up a deliverer for the people of Israel, who delivered them, Othniel the son of Kenaz,

Caleb's younger brother. The Spirit of the Lord came upon him, and he judged Israel." –Judges 3:9 KJV

Othniel was the only judge in the Scriptures from the tribe of Judah. The name literally means "lion of God," *Oth'ni-el*. Interestingly, Jesus is referred to as the "Lion of the Tribe of Judah."

After this first passage about the Spirit of the Lord coming upon a person, the term appears over ninety more times in the Scriptures, including eight times in the New Testaments.

Jesus reads a passage from Scripture before his townspeople in their synagogue, then sits down and states that "this passage is fulfilled that day." Some take this statement as the Grace of the Lord upon him, while others question who he thinks he is, because they know he is just the son of the carpenter Joseph.

"And he came to Nazareth, where he had been brought up; and he went to the synagogue, as his custom was, on the Sabbath day. And he stood up to read; and there was given to him the book of the prophet Isaiah. He opened the book and found the place where it was written: 'The Spirit of the Lord is upon me, because he has anointed me to preach good news to the poor. He has sent me to proclaim release to the captives and recovering of sight to the blind, to set at liberty those who are oppressed, to proclaim the acceptable year of the Lord.' And he closed the book, and gave it back to the attendant, and sat down; and the eyes of all in the synagogue were fixed on him. And he began to say to them, 'Today this scripture has been fulfilled in your hearing.'" (Luke 4:16-21)

Often Jesus stated that his powers, actions, and activities came from God the Father *within* him.

"The words that I say to you I do not speak on my own authority; but the Father who dwells in me does his works. Believe me that I am in the Father and the Father in me; or else believe me for the sake of the works themselves. Truly, truly, I say to you, he who believes in me will also do the works that I do; and greater works than these will he do, because I go to the Father." (John 14:10-12 RSV)

Later, in the garden just before his capture and crucifixion, he teaches that after he goes to the Father, he will send the "Spirit of Truth," who will be a comforter to us and teach us all things.

His term for this Spirit in the original Greek is *Paraclete*, which means counselor, helper, and comforter, and is considered by Christians to be the Spirit of God, the Spirit of the Lord, that will become our companion.

"I will pray the Father, and he will give you another Counselor, to be with you forever, even the Spirit of truth, whom the world cannot receive, because it neither sees him nor knows him; you know him, for he dwells with you, and will be in you. "I will not leave you desolate; I will come to you. Yet a little while, and the world will see me no more, but you will see me; because I live, you will live also. In that day you will know that I am in my Father, and you in me, and I in you." (John 14:16-20 RSV)

He adds to this, saying, "The Counselor, the Holy Spirit, whom the Father will send in my name, he will teach you all things, and bring to your remembrance all that I have said to you." (John 14:26 RSV)

Later in this teaching, he adds more about this Spirit, explaining that he, Jesus, has much more to say to us but we cannot take more now, so the Spirit will guide us.

"I have yet many things to say to you, but you cannot bear them now. When the Spirit of truth comes, he will guide you into all the truth; for he will not speak on his own authority, but whatever he hears he will speak, and he will declare to you the things that are to come." (John 16:12-13 RSV)

The disciple Paul adds another view into the nature of our consciousness and the Spirit of the Lord. There's a veil that needs to be removed so we can bear more of knowledge, more Spirit guidance.

"To this day whenever Moses is read a veil lies over their minds; but when a man turns to the Lord the veil is removed. Now the Lord is the Spirit, and where the Spirit of the Lord is, there is freedom. And we all, with unveiled face, beholding the glory of the Lord, are being changed into his likeness from one degree of glory to another; for this comes from the Lord who is the Spirit." (II Corinthians 3:15-18, RSV)

To the woman at the well, Jesus explained that "God is spirit, and those who worship him must worship in spirit and truth." (John 4:24 RSV) To Nicodemus, Jesus teaches that we have been born of flesh but we need to be born anew of Spirit.

"Truly, truly, I say to you, unless one is born of water and the Spirit, he cannot enter the kingdom of God. That which is born of the flesh is flesh, and that which is born of the Spirit is spirit. Do not marvel that I said to you, 'You must be born anew.' The wind blows where it wills, and you hear the sound of it, but you do not know whence it comes or whither it goes; so it is with every one who is born of the Spirit." (John 3:5-8 RSV)

When we practice the fruit of the Spirit, it nourishes us in a manner that gradually changes us from predominantly physical, worldly vibrations and consciousness to more spiritual, godly vibrations and consciousness. As one loves, one unites with love, and as the Scriptures point out: "God is love." (I John 4:8) As we apply these virtuous fruits in our thoughts, words, and actions each day, we become one with these virtues, thus united with the Spirit. Then the Spirit gives the gifts that strengthen us and that expand our minds and hearts in such a manner that we become increasingly one with God and companionable to God – the God of the entire universe and all that is in it. The evangelist Paul wrote:

"It is the Spirit himself bearing witness with our spirit that we are children of God." (Romans 8:16 RSV)

Edgar Cayce's discourses affirm this several times in various ways, here are two.

"Doubt not self, nor self's abilities, for in doing does strength come. Keep that consciousness that answers to self, as face answers to face in the water, and this will bring the answer in self as to whether the Spirit of the Creative Forces bears witness with your own spirit." (EC 262-7)

"Why is God mindful of an individual soul? Spirit! For our spirit, that is a portion of His Spirit, ever bears witness with His Spirit as to whether we be the children of God or not." (EC 262-115)

The Nature of Spirit

Just what is the nature of Spirit?

The word Spirit appears at the very beginning of the Bible, in the second verse of the first chapter of Genesis: "The Spirit of God moved upon the face of the waters." The actual Hebrew word used in this passage is *Ruwach*, which literally means "wind," as in "the wind of God moved upon the face of the waters." Wind is an unseen force behind a manifested condition. We see the leaves and branches of a tree move and we know the unseen wind is the cause.

Jesus picked up on this characteristic when he explained to Nicodemus the nature of the Spirit: "The wind blows where it will, and you hear the sound of it but do not know from where it comes or to where it goes; so is everyone who is born of the Spirit." (John 3:8) Now these words were written in Greek, and the Greek word here for Spirit is pneuma, which also means wind but has the added connotation of breath. Breath is personal wind; we inhale the Spirit of God and it become personal spirit within us. This is seen in the second chapter of Genesis when God breathes the breath of life into us and we become living souls. (Genesis 2:7)

Edgar Cayce also compared God to breath and wind: "God is but as the breath or the wind in its passing, yet in its passing may quicken ... each atom." (EC 1158-5)

Spirit is the life force. In the biblical book of Job, Elihu acknowledges that the Spirit has given life to us when he says, "the Spirit of God hath made me." (Job 33:4) God's Spirit gives life to all, including minerals, plants, and animals. Where there is Spirit, there is life.

In addition to life, the Spirit brings wisdom and understanding. Elihu states this in Job: "It is the Spirit in a man, the breath of the Almighty, that makes him understand." (Job 32:8-9) We also see how the Spirit brings wisdom when Pharaoh, after being astonished by Joseph's wisdom, asks his counselors, "Can we find such a man as this, in whom is the Spirit of God? Since God has shown you all this, there is none so discreet and wise as you are." (Gen. 41:38-39)

Spirit is the life force and brings enlightenment to our consciousness.

Here are three of Edgar Cayce's insights on the Spirit.

"God and the Christ Spirit is Life itself; and the motivating force of the soul is either for that companionship, that association, that development which will make such a soul-body as a fit companion for that Creative Influence manifested in the earth in Him, or it is for separating self from Him." (EC 524-2)

"Know ... an ideal must be beyond the purely material things in life, or in an experience in the earth. For these that are of the earth-earthy rust and corrupt. But those that are founded in the spirit of life and truth take hold upon the very throne of mercy and peace and harmony and justice and long-suffering and brotherly love; for they are of God—and thus are everlasting!" (EC 1125-1)

"Spirit is life, whether related to the physical functioning of the atomic forces within the system or whether that of the mental being of a body, and these must coordinate in the proper direction one with another, just as much as it is necessary for a physical functioning organ to coordinate with the rest of the system." (EC 2357-1)

The ultimate ecstasy is
"The liberation of the mind
from its finite consciousness,
becoming one
and identified with the Infinite."
–Plotinus (204–270 BC)
(the founder of Neo-Platonism, author of Enneads)

Chapter 8
The Infinite, Eternal Oneness

In the thousands of enlightening readings given by Edgar Cayce there is woven a fascinating thread telling of ancient beings who held a belief in the Oneness of all. As we study this idea in the Cayce archives, we become aware that Cayce is describing something much bigger than simple *oneness*, he's describing a *wholeness* from which no one can get beyond. No one can get beyond the Whole for the Whole is *the whole*; there is nothing beyond it. It is infinite and universal. Strangely, it is everywhere and yet nowhere! It is the Hidden Cosmic Womb *and* the Universe. Keep in mind that our scientists tell us that we only see 4% of the universe, 96% is invisible! There's much more to life and reality than we perceive at present. But there was a time when you and I knew it all! We experienced it all. And those memories are latent within us today.

Let's review this ancient tale in order to touch that place within us again. It begins long before our lives today. It begins when we were angels! Yes, we were once angels or "godlings" in the heart and mind of the Infinite Eternal One, as Kabbalah teaches. This is God and all of creation, what the Bible calls "the Heavenly Hosts" or "Heavenly Assembly." As we read earlier in this book, Jesus referred us to this passage in an answer he gave to the Pharisees in the gospel of John 10:34. The Pharisees charged him: "'It is not for a good work that we stone you but for blasphemy; because you, being a man, make yourself God." To this charge Jesus answered, "Is it not written in your law, 'I said, you are gods?'" Jesus is referring to lines in Psalm 82: "God presides in the great assembly. He judges among the gods. … You are gods, all of you are sons [and daughters] of the Most High."

According to Cayce and many other sources of ancient lore, you and I were conceived in the Universal Consciousness, in the Womb of God's Mind. It all began with God conceiving the essence of *beingness* or what is know today as the Logos, the prototype *being*. God is not a being but an infinite, eternal Spirit; as Jesus shared with the woman at the well: "God is Spirit and seeks same to worship Him." (John 4:24) And this Logos followed God's creative way by conceiving all of us—beings within *the* Being, which is in *the* Infinite Spirit. Jesus: "In that day you will know that I am in my Father, and you in me, and I in you." (John 14:20) And this Logos, or "the Word" as John wrote in the opening of his gospel, conceived us *intentionally* and *specifically!* Yes, I know it doesn't feel that way today, but it's true. And even today God, our Creator, is *mindful* of us; the Infinite is aware of each finite being. This is the Collective Consciousness within the Oneness.

Originally we were angels or godlings like God: "God created man in his own image. In God's image he created him; male and female he created them." (Genesis 1:26-27) The English word "man" in this passage is actually the Hebrew word for "being" or "person," with no gender-specific intimation. Male and female were one in each being. That word is "adam" with a lower-case "a", and does not mean a male man. And only in Genesis is this Hebrew word translated "man"; in other parts of the Bible this same word is translated as "person." The angels, godlings, or "persons" were created in the image of God, having both the yin and yang in oneness within themselves, as God also contains both. It was not until we get to Genesis, chapter 2, verse 18 that these qualities were separated into two different forms, woman and man.

In this next reading Cayce is being asked questions about angels and specifically the concept of a guardian angel: "Is it through the guardian angel that God speaks to the individual?" He answered: "Yes—through thy angel, through thy *self* that *is* the angel!—does the self speak with thy Ideal!" (1646-1) Here Cayce told his stenographer to italicize the words "self" and "is" in order to emphasize to us that a portion of *our* being *is* the angel! He also told her to capitalize the initial letter in the word "ideal" because it refers to God, but allows that we individuals have varying concepts of who and what God is, so Cayce allows for whatever our "ideal" of God maybe. In another reading he said: "The face of the self's *own* angel is ever before the Throne. Commune oft with Him." (1917-1) Can we accept this as absolutely true? Can we fully comprehend that a portion of you and me is "ever before the Throne" of God's consciousness? Clearly our original condition was as an angel and a godling, and that portion of us still exists, and it is that portion of our being that may commune with us, guard us, and even guide us because it is in direct contact with God's Mind, or another way to say this is that it is and has always been, and continues to be a portion of God! And it is through this angelic portion of our being that we may commune with our loving Creator, in whose image we are made and have our being.

Obviously we have come a long ways away from that origin. And yet, Cayce assures us that we retain this original spirituality within us. He says that when we first projected a *portion* of our consciousness into this world we retained the deep sense of oneness with the Infinite One. He even called us the "Children of the Law of One." Here's an example of the depths of his Oneness teachings: "The first lesson ... should be *One* - One - One - *One*; Oneness of God, oneness of man's relations, oneness of force, oneness of time, oneness of purpose, *Oneness* in every effort – Oneness - Oneness!" (900-429) When we look around today, we see multiplicity, diversity, and separateness. You are there. I am here. Your thoughts are yours; mine are mine. Oneness is not evident. Yet, from Edgar Cayce's spiritually motivated trance that connected him to the Universal Consciousness, he saw and taught oneness. For Cayce, our thoughts were *not* only ours because they affect the Collective Consciousness! In fact, when giving a reading he could tell *exactly* what we had been *thinking* because our thoughts left an impression upon the Universal Consciousness. And he could "read" these impressions. In fact, he could tell anyone of us what we *dreamed* last night even if we forgot! Thoughts for him were real "things"; so much so that during a reading he had difficulty determining if you or I had actually done something or just thought about doing it, because our thoughts made as strong an impression upon the Collective Consciousness as our actions! That's a scary thought! Oops, I just made another impression upon the Collective Consciousness! Cayce was desirous of us all grasping the implications of this unavoidable Oneness.

Is it possible that everyone and everything is a part of some unseen Collective, some indivisible Whole within which all the multiplicity exists, and each affects the composition of this Collective? Cayce says *yes*: "This is that portion of the lesson as is to be grounded into the inmost Self until all come to know that not only God is God ... for the self is a portion of that Oneness that may make itself a One with the Whole." (900-181) In several readings Cayce pressed us to simply believe this and live as if it were true! In this way we would come to know that it is indeed true. "Let this, my children, be the lesson for you: The intent in relating to each and every individual should be to bring forth that best element in each, in *oneness* of purpose, in oneness of spirit, in oneness of mind, towards each and every one that you contact—for the individuals, in the final analysis, are one." (288-19) In some manner that we don't readily perceive, all the individuals we meet and interact with each day, including ourselves, *are one*.

However, Cayce did acknowledge that the oneness had been broken by a "rebellion," and he stated that this rebellion began in the heavens, among the angels/godlings, long before the earth. And the rebellion was the result of selfish use of the God-given gift of free will. He teaches that God knew the potential for misuse and abuse of free will, and had prepared a universal law to govern it; that is the Law of Karma. This law is simple, whatever one does with their free will they experience. As the saying states: "What goes around, comes around." We meet the effects of our thoughts, words, and actions as they come back around to us. Maybe not in this life but eventually we will meet them again. This is not to punish or get revenge or retribution. No, this is to *educate* each free-willed being as to how their thoughts, words, and actions affect the Whole, the Oneness, the Collective—in hopes that they will choose more wisely the next time and subdue their self-centered, inconsiderate ways, and once again become cooperative in the Collective Oneness.

Here's an example of the angelic rebellion. He had given a reading in which an angelic being had spoken through him, and was later asked: "Who is Halaliel, the one who gave us a message on October 15th?" He answered: "One in and with whose courts Ariel fought when there was the rebellion in heaven. Now, where is heaven? Where is Ariel, and who was he? A companion of Lucifer or Satan, and one that made for the disputing of the influences in the experiences of Adam in the Garden." (EC 262-57) Now this is a perspective we are not used to, isn't it? Wow, there's a whole story we have lost touch with. Fortunately, Cayce is bringing it back to our remembrance. And since an important portion of our deeper being was *there*, we should review this legend.

The biblical prophet Isaiah gives us this: "How art thou fallen from heaven, O Lucifer, son of the morning! How art thou cut down to the ground, which didst weaken the nations! For thou hast said in thine heart, 'I will ascend into heaven, I will exalt my throne above the stars of God; I will sit also upon the mount of the congregation, in the sides of the north. I will ascend above the heights of the clouds; I will be like the most High.' Yet thou shalt be brought down to hell, to the sides of the pit." (Isaiah 14:12-15) As we can see, Lucifer got a little carried away with his role in the overall assembly of the Heaven Hosts. Cayce called this "self-exaltation, self-glorification," and he listed it among the abuses of free will. Lucifer personified this mistake. The name Lucifer means "the day star" or "morning star," also the planet Venus, or, as an adjective, "light-bringing." His name is often translated as "light bearer" or "light bringer." In fact, Lucifer is one of the three archangels mentioned in the Bible! And he was anointed as a guardian cherub as well! He was blameless from the day he was created, until unrighteousness was found in him. (Ezekiel 28:14,15) His light name becomes Satan, as indicated in Luke 10:18: "I saw Satan fall like lightning from heaven."

Now keeping the teaching of Oneness in mind we can see that even Lucifer/Satan cannot get out of the Whole, the Collective. He exists because God allows it. This is revealed in the parable of the sower: "The kingdom of heaven may be compared to a man who sowed good seed in his field; but while men were sleeping, his enemy came and sowed weeds among the wheat, and went away. So when the plants came up and bore grain, then the weeds appeared also. And the servants of the householder came and said to him, 'Then do you want us to go and gather the weeds?' But he said, 'No; lest in gathering the weeds you root up the wheat along with them.'" (Matthew 13:24-30) God allows the darkness to exist with the light.

Surprisingly, even Lucifer can redeem himself. This is the magic of the Law of Karma. Whatever goes around comes around. Thus, as a being changes what they are projecting, their karma changes. As one begins to consider others rather than just oneself, consideration comes back upon that person. As one understands mistakes, one's mistakes are understood. As one forgives what others have said or done, what one has said or done is forgiven. The law is perfect. Lucifer, as the light of Venus (love), misused his free will and became Satan, the light of Saturn (the challenger)—the ancient Persians actually called the planet "Satan." Satan means "the adversary, one who rebels or resist" and is often considered "the accuser or challenger" because of how God allowed Satan to test Job to see if Satan's accusation against Job was true: "If you touch one thing of his physical life, he'll curse you to your face," indicating that Job was not in love with God and Spirituality, no, he loved his physical possessions and life, and nothing more. Of course Job proved Satan wrong, and ultimately communed with

179

God and received a hundred fold of what he had lost during the test.

Cayce prophesied that our life will come full circle around again, and we will regain the awareness we had, oh so long ago. And not only the awareness, we will regain the ability to *affect* life using our free wills, even to control Nature and change matter and energy. But he warned that we had these abilities once and misused them, so how will we use them when they come around again? (1602-3, Q&A 19, 20, and 21) We are the Children of the Law of One, the Morning Stars that sang together as recorded in the biblical book of Job 38:7. Can we act and think like it? That is the question.

Egyptian symbol "Ra Mess" meaning *born of God*,
as in the name *Ramses*, which is more correctly
spelled *Ramesses*, "one born of God."
We all, our souls, are *Ra Mess*.

APPENDIX

Source Notes for Chapter 1
These are the Cayce file numbers.
1 One good example is 254-67.
2 #137-5
3 #294-140
4 #900-10
5 #137-5
6 two examples are #294-103 & -155
7 John 4:24
8 Bits and pieces found in 294-103 & -140, 900-16, 1033-1, 3744-1 through -4, 5756-4, and several others.
9 #3744-1
10 #294-4
11 #3744-2
12 #900-10
13 #254-67
14 See also Sleep and the Sixth Sense in the next section.
15 Rev. 1:10-12, #281-16
16 3976-14
17 254-67 Report but the explanation is in 254-68 Reading.
18 For some examples see 2995-1, 2420-1, and 3351-1.
19 #3744-1
20 Luke 1:35
21 "As to their forms in the physical sense, these were much rather of the nature of THOUGHT FORMS, or able to push out OF THEMSELVES in that direction in which its development took shape in thought - much in the way and manner as the amoeba would in the waters

of a stagnant bay, or lake, in the present." 364-3
paragraph 5.
22 #3744-2
23 #900-16, my italics
24 #3744-1, 2 & 4
25 #281-5
26 #262-87
27 #294-19, 254-68
28 3744-1, 4648-1
29 see 254-48, 4648-1, and 5640-1
30 5640-1, 600-1, 4648-1 and others.
31 262-15, 294-140, and 5754-1 and -3.
32 900-461

John Van Auken
P.O. Box 4942
Virginia Beach, VA 23454

John@JohnVanAuken.com
JohnVanAuken.com

You may email a request for a free
review copy of John's newsletter
at the above email address.
John's speaking, touring, and online-course schedule is
posted on the web site above.

Other Books by John Van Auken
(all available through Amazon.com)

• *Edgar Cayce and the Kabbalah: A Resource for Soulful Living.* with 30 illustrations, A.R.E Press, 2010.

• *Edgar Cayce's Amazing Interpretation of the Revelation*, with 44 illustrations, Living in the Light, 2015.

• *A Broader View of Jesus Christ*, Living in the Light, 2015.

• *Hidden Teachings of Jesus*, Living in the Light, 2015.

• *Reincarnation & Karma: Our Soul's Past-Life Influences*, Living in the Light, 2015.

• *Edgar Cayce on the Spiritual Forces Within You*, A.R.E. Press, 2014.

• *Toward a Deeper Meditation*, A.R.E. Press, 2007.

• *From Karma to Grace*, A.R.E. Press, 2010.

• *Angels, Fairies, Demons, and the Elementals: With the Edgar Cayce Perspective on the Supernatural World*, A.R.E. Press, 2015.

• *Edgar Cayce on the Reincarnated Essenes*, A.R.E. Press, 2016.

• *2038 – Great Pyramid Timeline Prophecy*, A.R.E. Press, 2012.

• *Edgar Cayce's Tales of Egypt*, A.R.E. Press, 2011.

• *Ancient Egyptian Mysticism*, A.R.E. Press, 1999.

• *Edgar Cayce's Atlantis*, A.R.E. Press, 2006.

Made in the USA
Columbia, SC
03 May 2023

16062200R00104